HIGH STAKES

HIGH STAKES

The Rising Cost of
America's Gambling Addiction

Sam Skolnik

Beacon Press
Boston

BEACON PRESS
25 Beacon Street
Boston, Massachusetts 02108-2892
www.beacon.org

Beacon Press books
are published under the auspices of
the Unitarian Universalist Association of Congregations.

14 13 12 11   8 7 6 5 4 3 2 1

This book is printed on acid-free paper that meets the uncoated paper
ANSI/NISO specifications for permanence as revised in 1992.

Text design by Yvonne Tsang at Wilsted & Taylor Publishing Services

The names of a few people mentioned in this work
have been changed to protect their identities. In each case
where an alias has been used, it has been noted in the text.

Library of Congress Cataloging-in-Publication Data

Skolnik, Sam.
High stakes : the rising cost of America's gambling addiction / Sam Skolnik.
p. cm.
Includes bibliographical references and index.
ISBN 978-0-8070-0629-0 (hbk. : alk. paper) 1. Gambling—United States.
2. Compulsive gambling—Social aspects—United States.
3. Gambling industry—United States. I. Title.
HV6715.S56 2011
362.2'5—dc22   2010050222

To my parents

and

To all the gamblers out there,
including those in recovery

Axel: Double it.
Dealer: You want to double on eighteen, sir?
Axel: Yes. Give me the three.

—Axel Freed in *The Gambler*, written by James Toback (1974)

CONTENTS

A Gambler's Journey, and a Country's

I started gambling seriously in 2000, the year I moved to Seattle for a newspaper job. By 2001, I was hooked. I've been grappling with a poker addiction ever since.

While I've had some happier times at the poker tables recently, during the past decade gambling has often wreaked havoc with my life. I don't know if I've "hit bottom"—a term many in the recovery community rightly detest—because I don't know what, for me, bottom is.

There are things I've never done because of my habit. I've never borrowed from a loan shark or bet with a bookie. I've never stolen anything to raise gambling funds. I've never missed filing my taxes. I've never been kicked out of my apartment because I couldn't pay the rent—though God knows how many times I've been days and even weeks late. I've never let work slide so badly that it caused me to be fired.

But there are lots of ways in which my gambling affected me for the worse during my six years in Seattle and more recently in Las Vegas:

I've left bills unpaid, sometimes for weeks, months, or years. I've had credit cards canceled and had creditors harass me with phone calls at all hours, sometimes leaving me screaming at the walls.

I've borrowed incessantly, both to raise poker funds and to pay bills. I borrowed at least five times against my old 1991 Miata, in the end, undoubtedly borrowing much more than the car was actually worth. I've borrowed simultaneously from five different payday loan stores in Seattle and later from four in Las Vegas—all at usurious rates.

Several times when the losses mounted and funds were especially tight, I've survived for days on end on boxes of store-brand mac and cheese, ramen noodles, saltines, and seltzer water.

I've never been arrested, but I have been pulled over by police several times in Washington and Nevada because of expired license plate tabs. In Vegas, where the utility companies don't mess around, I've had both my phone service and my power briefly shut off.

There have been instances when I've been less productive at work than I needed to be. And I'm not as ambitious—or I should say, I'm not as ambitious with regard to my journalism career—as I used to be or still ought to be. My career dreams have largely shifted from Pulitzer Prizes to World Series of Poker gold bracelets.

Perhaps worst of all, I've been missing out on some basic human connections. I've let some friendships and family relationships wither, and I've surely missed making new friends. And I've dated and pursued serious girlfriends less energetically than I used to. Some of that might be a function of impending middle age, but much of it, without doubt, is due to poker.

I still play, but I don't know what my gambling future holds. It's my hope that I'll be able to find a way to reinvigorate my life through reduced time at the poker tables. Quitting for good is one option and is something I recognize may ultimately be the answer. To do that, Gamblers Anonymous undoubtedly will need to be a big part of the equation. Another option is to do nothing, to continue to play regularly, no matter where I live. After all, it's becoming more and more difficult to find a region of the country not within easy driving distance from a legal poker room. Regardless of where I end up—

and I'm thinking staying in Las Vegas is not the answer for me, for many reasons on top of the ubiquitous gambling—I just can't envision this option B being a palatable long-term choice.

I'm currently leaning toward a third option, one espoused by two writers who each released gambling memoirs in the last few years, Martha Frankel and Burt Dragin. Both had developed serious gambling problems—Frankel through Internet poker (something that thankfully has never held much appeal for me) and Dragin through regular trips to casinos. Neither ended up in recovery. Instead, both say their answer has been to limit their gambling to a weekly poker game with friends and reasonable stakes.

"[T]his game is social and relaxing, not compulsive and fearful," wrote Frankel, a celebrity profiler for magazines, in her 2008 book *Hats & Eyeglasses: A Family Love Affair with Gambling.* "It reminds me of the fun that I had when I first started playing, and how much I love poker. And it shows me that I'm no longer out of control, fighting a dragon I could never slay."

Maybe this kind of solution could work for me, with a trip or two to Vegas every year tacked on for good measure. Maybe it's pie-in-the-sky thinking. I don't yet know.

It's not easy to write these things. There's a certain shame attached to confessing a gambling addiction in our culture, even more so than copping to being an alcoholic or a cocaine addict. Many still believe that people gamble excessively because of a lack of willpower or because they're simply immoral. These antiquated beliefs are beginning to fade, as doctors, scientists, and researchers are increasingly concluding that pathological gambling is a behavioral addiction that affects the brain in much the same way as substance dependencies. I share this notion.

Though research suggests that about one in two problem gamblers suffer other types of addictions, I don't. Except for maybe a few beers a week, I don't drink. Illegal drugs generally scare the daylights out of me. Pot doesn't, but I haven't taken a toke in more than a decade and have no interest in it. I drink less coffee and Diet Coke than your standard card-carrying reporter, and I've never touched tobacco aside from the rare cigar. Except for an unhealthy fondness for thin-crust pepperoni pizza, I'm not a food addict, nor do I shop, spend, work, or have sex anywhere near too much. For me, it's just about the gambling.

I'm not sharing this highly personal information because this book is about me. It isn't. But my perspective has been shaped by my experiences inside casinos and poker rooms, as well as the recovery meetings I've attended sporadically over the years in church basements and community centers. Readers deserve to know my history on the topic.

Certainly, but for my habit, I never would have pursued writing this book.

Yet if anything, I'm even more interested in the topic as a reporter. Several years ago while living in Seattle, I realized there was an important, untold story about the rise of problem gambling in Washington state. Over the last twenty years, several regional newspapers have chronicled how sudden infusions of gambling have impacted their cities and states. I wrote one of those accounts in 2004, in a three-day, front-page series for the *Seattle Post-Intelligencer.*

Ever since, I've felt that a book urgently needed to be written that investigated the consequences of our gambling boom—how we, as a nation, are in many ways gambling with our collective future. Studies suggest there are likely millions out there like me—people who have gotten caught up in gambling's grip, mostly or entirely as a result of the spread of legalized gambling over the last several decades. These numbers include many who never would have developed gambling problems if casinos and other gambling businesses hadn't been allowed to plant themselves in their communities.

And yet, incredibly to me, no one to date has written this larger national tale, at least not since 1995, when author Robert Goodman published his critically acclaimed treatise called *The Luck Business: The Devastating Consequences and Broken Promises of America's Gambling Explosion.* Since then, legalized gambling throughout America has only grown—exponentially.

America has always been a nation of gamblers, from the colonial era horse race bettors to the nineteenth-century Mississippi riverboat card sharks, all the way to the millions who now annually pay homage to the garish gambling temples of the Las Vegas Strip.

Since the 1970s, however, legalized gambling has grabbed hold of the country's consciousness in a way it never before has. It's rooted itself in scores of cities and small towns in every region, from Albuquerque to Detroit, including many that never before have had to deal directly with the fallout.

Native American tribes have renegotiated compacts in more than two dozen states to allow for new casinos. State governments have joined in, bringing private casinos, card rooms, and video poker and slot machines by the tens of thousands into their jurisdictions.

The national poker craze has proved amazingly durable. Consider the game's exposure on television. During just one week in May 2010, fifty-eight episodes of fourteen different poker tournaments or cash games ran on eight different networks. By contrast, as of the mid-1990s, a single network broadcast just one hour-long poker show per year on TV.

Internet gambling is still on the rise although Congress has deemed it quasi-illegal. Forty-three states, the District of Columbia, Puerto Rico, and the U.S. Virgin Islands each sponsor heavily promoted lotteries.

In 2007, Americans lost more than $92 billion gambling[1]—about nine times what they lost in 1982.[2] To put that amount into perspective, it's almost ten times what moviegoers in the United States spent on tickets during the same year.[3]

In 2005, 73 million Americans were estimated to have patronized one of the country's twelve hundred casinos, card rooms, or bingo parlors—twenty million more than just five years earlier.[4]

Thirty-five years ago, casinos were legal in one state, Nevada. As of 2010, various forms of gambling have been legalized everywhere in the United States except Utah and Hawaii. The majority of Americans now live within a three- to four-hour drive of a casino.

The total amount wagered legally in the United States is "undoubtedly well over" a trillion dollars per year, one of the nation's leading gambling experts concluded in 2010.[5] Because of this growth, millions of Americans have for the first time been directly exposed to gambling. As a result, there's been a significant increase in the number of addicted gamblers around the country. There is a fairly obvious proposition at work here: in communities where legalized gambling has been introduced, new problem and pathological gamblers have been forged.

According to experts, gambling becomes a problem when it disrupts or damages personal lives or careers. Problem gamblers often devolve into pathological gamblers when the gambler loses control over her betting; when she gambles more often or for larger amounts; and perhaps most importantly, when she continues to gamble despite adverse consequences.

Those consequences are felt not just by the gamblers. They ripple outward to family and friends, employers and whole communities. They run the gamut from decreased work productivity and increased physical and mental health problems to rises in divorces and various types of crimes, from theft and embezzlement to domestic violence and child abuse. Studies have also shown that pathological gambling has caused an increase in bankruptcy filings and claims for unemployment and welfare benefits, and in the worst cases, suicides.

The gambling industry[6] argues that in the long run, problem gambling rates in some communities where gambling has been introduced have stayed about the same or have even decreased slightly. In certain cases this may be true, as some who initially develop problems because of the new availability of gambling subsequently undergo what researchers call an "adaptation" effect. Though problem gambling rates almost always spike immediately after the introduction of legalized gambling, sometimes they slowly drop back to where they were—presumably in large part because invigorated public awareness campaigns, telephone help lines, and professional treatment and counseling programs have helped stem the damage. But this misses several important points. In the worst cases, many gamblers "adapt" by going to jail or committing suicide. Regardless, even in communities where adaptation may have occurred, it's always the case that an initial spike in problem gambling rates means a greater number of injured lives, temporary or not. Finally, many researchers discount the adaptation thesis, concluding that legalizing gambling, especially slot machines, results in problem gambling rates that, over time, remain higher than they were and do not wane to a large degree, a topic I address in the upcoming chapter on gambling research and science.

Indeed, the most noteworthy research conducted over the last couple of decades concludes that the unremitting expansion of legalized gambling has helped turn great numbers of Americans into problem and pathological gamblers.

To wit:

A comprehensive "meta-analysis" of one hundred and twenty gambling prevalence research studies, which looked at gambling behavior in the United States and Canada between 1974 and 1997, concluded that there had been a dramatic rise in the adult problem and pathological gambling rates over that time. While the studies conducted from 1977 to 1993 determined that at some point over their lifetimes, 4.38 percent of the two countries' general populations had become problem or pathological gamblers, the 1994 to 1997 studies showed a sharp hike in the percentage of "lifetime" problem or pathological gamblers—more than 2 percent, to nearly 7 percent. That's a jump of more than 4.3 million people—roughly equivalent to the entire populations of states such as Kentucky or Louisiana.

"As gambling has become more socially accepted and accessible during the past two decades," adults in the general population have "started to gamble in increasing numbers," the study concluded. It was led by Howard Shaffer, the Harvard-affiliated and gambling industry–funded researcher who later helped develop the adaptation theory. "Newly exposed to the gambling experience, adults in the general population are having difficulty adjusting and, unlike the other population segments who already evidence gambling problems, are beginning to report increasingly higher rates of gambling disorder."[7]

Other prominent studies back up this notion. The gambling behavior survey carried out for the National Gambling Impact Study Commission[8] determined that those who lived within fifty miles of a casino were more than twice as likely to develop significant problems as those who lived between fifty and two hundred and fifty miles from the establishment. Within the fifty-mile zone, the pathological gambling rate was 2.1 percent; outside it, it was 0.9 percent. This conclusion—that proximity to gambling venues spurs higher problem gambling rates—has since been supported repeatedly by other independent studies.[9]

And look at the rates of both problem and pathological gambling in Nevada—by far the most extensive legalized gambling market in the United States. They far outstrip the rest of the country. The most complete prevalence survey ever taken in Nevada, published in 2002, showed that the incidence of problem and pathological gambling in Nevada was exponentially higher than in the United States as a whole.

The study concluded that 2.9 percent of the state's adult population were problem gamblers, and that another 3.5 percent were "probable" pathological gamblers—for a whopping total of 6.4 percent of the population.[10] Assuming that those rates have remained the same, given Nevada's 2010 population, that amounts to more than one hundred and fifteen thousand adults.

Spend any time in Las Vegas and it's easy to conclude that those numbers, if anything, are an understatement. The number of pawn shops and payday loan stores that mark virtually every neighborhood—places for often-desperate problem gamblers to replenish their gambling bankrolls—is astonishing. As a resident, you can't escape gambling. Not only have "locals casinos" sprouted up in every corner of the Las Vegas Valley, not only are casino promotions plastered on countless billboards throughout the region and on TV and radio advertisements, it's nearly impossible to grab a drink at a neighborhood bar or even shop for groceries or buy gasoline without passing by banks of slots and video poker machines. It's a phenomenon I'll be exploring in an upcoming chapter.

What's more, it's clear that as the number and range of legalized gambling opportunities have grown throughout Las Vegas—and the country—and as a rising number of gamblers have suffered serious consequences, more and more have turned to Gamblers Anonymous, or GA, for help.

Over a recent ten-year period, GA—a twelve-step support program modeled after Alcoholics Anonymous—grew dramatically. From 1996 to 2005, the number of weekly GA meetings nationwide rose by almost 50 percent, from 1,073 to 1,584.

I found even more stark numbers when I wrote my newspaper series in Seattle. In the decade preceding that series, gambling revenues in Washington state had tripled, from $437 million in 1994 to $1.31 billion a decade later. (The most recent annual count for fiscal 2009 showed gambling revenues in the state were more than $2.1 billion.) Meantime, during that same ten-year period, the number of GA chapters in western Washington had grown seven-fold, from four to twenty-eight. The average size of each meeting had also more than doubled.

Yet the newly addicted gamblers and all those they impact aren't the only victims. States and other municipalities have also increasingly been suffering some pretty severe gambling hangovers. Governors, state legislators, and mayors all around the country have become hooked on gambling revenue, coveting the easy ways the steady stream of government gambling winnings have shored up budget deficits, paid for education programs, and reduced property and income taxes.

Gambling revenues have become critical income streams for more than a few state governments. According to a 2005 report released by researchers at the University of Nevada, Las Vegas, in four states—Louisiana, Nevada, Oregon, and South Dakota—taxes from casinos, slot machines, video poker terminals, racetracks, and states lotteries made up more than 10 percent of overall revenues. In six other states, gambling brought in more than 6 percent of overall revenues, and the numbers are growing rapidly.

State leaders don't relinquish these income streams easily. And in many states, officials are clamoring for more gambling. In 2009 and 2010, officials in thirty-seven states—three out of four—pushed for new or expanded gambling. The evidence is clear that the gambling industry and their politician partners are gearing up for more battles than ever, recession or not. As the recession took root, in fact, leaders of many states with some forms of legalized gambling urged voters to approve more. This has been a bright spot for gambling operators hit like other businesses by the economic downturn.

Look at Pennsylvania. In 2004, at the urging of Governor Ed Rendell, legislators allowed for sixty-one thousand slot machines, more than in any other state east of Nevada, to operate in horse tracks, resorts, and slot parlors across the state. They've been a hit. In April 2010, the nine slot machine facilities operating in Pennsylvania collectively generated $195 million in gross revenues—an increase of 30 percent over the $150 million generated in April 2009, when two fewer slot casinos were in operation.

In December 2009, slot machine revenues in Pennsylvania for the first time surpassed those in Atlantic City, traditionally the East Coast's preeminent gambling stronghold.[11]

The following month, Rendell signed a bill legalizing table games such as blackjack, roulette, and poker. State leaders promised that the action would bring in $250 million in new gambling tax revenue for the state, create jobs, and allow them to avert layoffs of state workers. But Rendell and his allies still weren't finished. Three months later, in April 2010, a state legislator announced he was drafting legislation to legalize video lottery machines that would feature video poker—games that some critics have suggested are the "crack cocaine of gambling"—which could be placed in bars and restaurants.

"There is not a desire to raise gas taxes. There is not a desire to raise any other taxes or to raise (vehicle) registration fees," the sponsor, Representative Paul Costa, told the *Patriot-News* of Harrisburg. "So this is a way to raise revenue without raising taxes."[12]

Other legislators bristled at the idea, arguing that placing the machines in taverns and restaurants would lead to more gambling addiction and change the character of neighborhoods. "Video poker is probably the worst public policy idea that's been advanced in Pennsylvania in a generation," said Senate Majority Leader Dominic Pileggi.[13]

Such debates are being hashed out all over the country, as I detail later in the book. Yet as more states are seeking to expand gambling, legislators at the same time are taking less responsibility for the problem and pathological gamblers they've helped create. According to a March 2010 Associated Press story: "In many states, the funds for helping problem gamblers have been cut sharply because of the budget problems."[14]

Few politicians are demanding that existing casinos be dismantled or state lotteries disbanded. But increasing numbers in both parties are starting to recognize—as the congressionally mandated National Gambling Impact Study Commission urged in 1999—that perhaps it's time again to consider a "pause" in plans for further gambling expansion.[15]

"Without a pause and reflection the future does indeed look worrisome," the commission concluded. "Were one to use the experience of the last quarter century to predict the evolution of gambling over the next, a likely scenario would be for gambling to continue to become more and more common, ultimately omnipresent in our lives and those of our children, with consequences no one can profess to know."

This is a book about the rise of legalized gambling and the culture it is creating in big cities and small towns across the nation. That Pennsylvania pol has it right: gambling changes the character of communities in ways other businesses do not—and has many types of impacts, from the economic and political to the scientific, medical, sociological, and cultural.

The book will be told through the stories of politicians and activists, medical and mental health professionals, and gambling industry officials—and, of course, through the problem gamblers in our midst, recovering or not, and the people they've affected.

These gamblers include poker players like me. Many players, including so-called "professionals," resent being lumped in with other gamblers. Poker is primarily a game of skill, they argue, and not a game played against the house like blackjack, craps, or roulette, which cannot be beaten over the long haul.

Indeed, there are winning poker players—meaning those who are able not only to beat the game regularly, but who also have the discipline to manage their money well and who aren't addicted to other casino games, unaffordable lifestyles, or drugs. But they are truly uncommon, a much rarer phenomenon than overhyped poker magazines, TV shows, and advertisements would lead most to believe. And poker players are every bit as susceptible to becoming addicted as other gamblers. I'll be discussing the poker boom and the related rise of Internet gambling in more depth in two upcoming chapters.

The evolution of how problem gamblers have been recognized in American society has been driven in large part by how the condition is viewed among scientists and doctors. Long classified as an "impulse control disorder"—closer to kleptomania or pyromania than to alcoholism—leading psychiatrists and addiction researchers are set soon to change their definition. In its 2013 *Diagnostic and Statistical Manual of Mental Disorders*, called the *DSM-V*, the American Psychiatric Association is ready to reclassify pathological gambling as a "behavioral addiction" more akin neurologically to alcohol and drug addictions. This is further evidence that it is being accepted as a valid medical condition as opposed to a moral failing. (The *DSM-V* also will begin replacing the term "pathological gambling" with "disordered gambling." This book, however—following the lead of the vast majority of independent studies conducted from the mid-1990s through 2010—will stick with the terms "problem" and "pathological gambling.")

The chapter on gambling science also will look at problem gambling research—and the way the gambling industry has cornered much of the research market through the National Center for Responsible Gaming (NCRG), the nonprofit research arm of the American Gaming Association (AGA), the powerful trade group for the commercial casino industry. The NCRG funds the majority of the problem gambling research conducted in the United States and is or has been affiliated with several top medical schools, including those at Harvard and Yale. This has prompted concerns among critics who assert that the industry is in effect attempting to buy research legitimacy and conclusions that suit its purposes—that gambling is less addictive than many believe; that pathological gamblers frequently have addictive personalities and substance abuse issues, implying that the industry should in no way be held to blame for their gambling addiction; that living close to a gambling facility doesn't lead to higher gambling addiction rates; that problem gamblers don't provide the industry with the high percentage of overall revenues that numerous independent studies have suggested.

Of course it's in the industry's interest to present a narrative that allows for continued legalization and growth. But critics contend that involves regularly distorting the truth. "The industry's ability to downplay the social costs has been a continual frustration," Henry Lesieur, a psychologist with the Rhode Island Hospital's gambling treatment program, told Salon.com in 2008. "As if one suicide isn't too many, or as if divorces mean very little."[16]

Some independent observers have long suggested that one way to combat the dominant stream of industry-funded research would be for the federal government to step in and provide research funding through the National Institutes of Health. In fact, as of October 2010, Congress was considering the Comprehensive Problem Gambling Act, which would fund $20 million in federally funded research grants and another $50 million for problem gambling treatment and prevention over a five-year period. When asked to support a similar bill in 2007, the NCRG declined. In May 2010, a spokeswoman for the group said the NCRG does not take positions on legislation or public policy. But in a written statement provided by AGA communications director Holly Thomsen, the casino trade group made it clear it won't be supporting the 2010 bill. It's "not the most effective approach" to address the issue, according to the statement. "Without a thorough needs assessment, the bill has the potential to add an additional layer of bureaucracy and additional expense to current efforts that have been effective at limiting pathological gambling to approximately 1 percent of the adult population."

Problem gambling researchers have long noticed that specific demographic groups—including the young and the elderly—are especially at risk for developing gambling problems. But there's another group in American society that deserves a closer inspection, especially as the gambling industry has been targeting them as customers: Asian-Americans, the fastest-growing racial or ethnic group in the country for the last decade. Asian-Americans, especially those of Chinese, Vietnamese, and Korean descent, gamble at higher rates than Americans from other ethnic backgrounds. They suffer as problem gamblers at higher rates, too. Repeated studies have yielded some shocking results. The gambling industry knows this—and appears to be doing everything it can to exploit it, from buses that stream daily into Chinatowns all over the country to take Asian gamblers to play, to targeted advertisements sent to Asian customers, to specially designed casino floors, restaurants, and entertainment options with Asian themes.

"This marketing goes beyond targeting and into predatory practices," said Helen Gym, a Philadelphia-based Asian community activist, in my chapter on Asian gambling. "We consider it to be a devastating thing."

I don't mean to propose that legalized gambling is responsible for every social ill befalling America. Far from it. Gambling businesses provide jobs—something that can't be scoffed at, especially in the bottomed-out economy we're suffering through as I write this book. And in many states, gambling revenues provide tax relief and funding for public education that is of clear benefit to communities, especially poorer ones.

Not to mention, a significant majority of those who visit their nearby racetrack or Indian casino or video poker bar with friends once or twice a month, or who buy the occasional lottery ticket with dreams of striking it rich, do so without developing negative side effects. They don't gamble because they're addicted. They simply get a kick out of it, and they're glad the state has provided them with the entertainment option.

And yet.

The gambling boom has had myriad consequences—costs that have grown right alongside the industry's growth. I'm writing this book to raise awareness of these costs. In the end, voters in more and more states are being asked to weigh whether to grant gambling a place in their communities and possibly their lives. They need to know the real price of gambling's bright neon lights.

CHAPTER I

The Other Gambling Addicts: The States

JoDean Joy, a housewife and mother of five who grew up on a farm outside Miller, South Dakota, became the state's leading citizen-activist against gambling for an understandable reason: it had caused anguish to those close to her. Her son-in-law, an Iowa accountant named Bob Phillips, had embezzled millions of dollars from clients to support his gambling addiction. Phillips's crimes had a devastating impact on her daughter's family. The incident also began to steel Joy to the notion that she needed to fight legalized gambling, a growing force in her home state.

Joy's metamorphosis into what one friend would call "the pit bull of Miller"[1] took two years. It was completed as she lay in a hospital bed in 1991, recuperating from surgery and listening to a TV news report of a poll that found 83 percent of South Dakotans wanted to get rid of video lottery terminals, the slotlike machines that had flooded the state's bars, restaurants, and convenience stores two years before. The report also quoted former governor Bill Janklow calling the vote to approve the machines "the dumbest damn thing" the state had ever done. As she listened, she became more and more riled. She knew how gambling could wound a family. She had to act.

Joy had noticed lots of changes after gambling exploded in South Dakota in 1989, the year she'd learned of Phillips's crimes. None were improvements. There were the stories she heard from teachers about students no longer having money for new clothes or even meals because their parents had gambled away their paychecks. There was a friend of hers, a banker who had skimmed money off of her clients' accounts in order to rush back to the video lottery terminals. There were business owners injured by decreased sales and unpaid debts. And these were just her hometown examples. "In a very small town, it's impossible to get away from them," she said, referring to the lottery machines. "It ruins the fabric of society."

Over the next two decades, Joy has traveled her state and worked with antigambling activists from around the country, trying to fight the push for ever more state-sponsored gambling. One of her first battles was the highest profile gambling fight South Dakota had ever seen—and the result was a shocker. Joy and her modest group of supporters took on a movie star and won. In 1993, the state legislature voted to increase the number of gaming devices in Deadwood, the Black Hills town that had legalized casinos a few years before. The measure also raised the betting limits from $5 to $100. Joy got a referendum on the ballot to repeal the law and won with 55 percent of the vote, despite being outspent by an eight to one margin.[2] One of the main lobbyists against the referendum was the actor Kevin Costner. Though Costner owns another Deadwood casino called the Midnight Star, he and his brother Dan Costner wanted to open a $100-million casino resort called the Dunbar, named after his character in his Oscar-winning *Dances with Wolves*, which was set in the state. The Dunbar would have dwarfed the other casinos in the town. But after the referendum passed, the brothers halted work on the project.

Joy, seventy-five when we spoke, and her allies have lost more battles than they've won since then—including their inability to reverse the legislature's repeat action in 2000 to increase the Deadwood casinos' betting limits. Joy said she's trying to look forward and occasionally still writes letters to local newspapers about gambling's dangers. She has straightforward advice to voters and officials in other states weighing whether to expand gambling. "I tell them, if you care anything for the well-being of the citizens of your state, you have to fight against it."

Before 1989, South Dakota was a different kind of place. Deadwood, infamous in its early days for prostitution, opium smoking, and general lawlessness spurred by the 1875 Gold Rush, epitomized by Wild Bill Hickok, Calamity Jane, and the like, had by then mellowed into a sleepy tourist town of two thousand. Indian casinos hadn't yet begun sprouting up in most corners of the sparse Great Plains landscape, drawing gamblers from every region of the state. And there were no video lottery terminals.

Two decades since these gambling businesses all were legalized, South Dakota and many of its citizens have become hooked on gambling. Deadwood now boasts more than two dozen casinos. The establishments collectively managed to earn total gross revenues of just over $100 million in fiscal year 2009—three times the revenues earned in 1991.[3] The profits produced by South Dakota's nine Indian casinos are not publicly known. They follow the lead of the National Indian Gaming Commission, which says it "does not make tribal-specific or state-specific confidential financial information available to the public." But according to a 2004 report sponsored by the South Dakota Commission on Gaming, the state's Indian casinos generated about $75 million in profits in the previous year.[4] (As of late 2010, a tenth Indian casino in the state, to be located in the Sioux Falls area, was in the planning stages. It was proposed to compete with a $120 million commercial casino being built just over the Iowa border.)

The biggest gambling industry earner is the state lottery, predominantly through its 9,018 video lottery terminals spread throughout 1,388 bars, restaurants, and special rooms with liquor licenses that are tacked onto convenience stores. In 2009, the machines, which like Vegas-style slots offer video poker, blackjack, keno, and bingo, netted $219 million.[5] By law, half of that video lottery revenue goes to the state. The percentage forwarded to the state used to be much less; legislators have boosted their share five times since 1989.

In fact, South Dakota is more dependent on its gambling revenue than every state but one. In the mid-2000s, two different researchers pegged gambling revenues as making up between 13 and 18 percent of the state's overall budget—second in its reliance on gambling profits only to Nevada.[6] The state's video lottery proceeds go almost entirely toward property tax reduction. Millions in additional winnings from scratch and lotto tickets go toward the state's general fund, half of which is used to support public education, from elementary schools to state universities.

The benefits of legalized gambling in the state have outweighed the drawbacks, said Bob Hartford, executive director of the Music and Vending Association of South Dakota, which represents the vendors who maintain and lease the video gambling machines. And not just because of the reduced taxes and the entertainment option they provide to nonaddicted gamblers. The video lottery has resulted in four thousand jobs, and Deadwood casinos have provided another twenty-five hundred, he said. "I think South Dakota has become more prosperous," he said. The notion that the machines have had a detrimental effect on the culture is ridiculous, he added. Reporters may be quick to tell stories of gamblers who've ruined their lives after becoming hooked on the machines, but a pair of reports conducted in the 1990s backs the notion that problem gambling rates and resulting social costs haven't risen, he said.

Yet a range of data points to a different conclusion. Within two years of legalized gambling's spread throughout the state, gambling addiction had suddenly become one of the leading causes of personal and business bankruptcy filings, a newspaper report found.[7] Before 1989, bankruptcies in the state were almost never caused by gambling. Another indicator of a sustained problem is the number of Gamblers Anonymous chapters in South Dakota—thirty. This number is almost twice as high as the sixteen GA meetings held weekly in North Dakota—a state with a fraction of South Dakota's legalized gambling but 80 percent of its population.

Jeff Bloomberg was the state's attorney for Lawrence County, which includes Deadwood, from 1986 to 1995. A year before he left office, he testified before a congressional committee that statistics from his office showed there had been an increase in reported child abuse and neglect cases since the Deadwood casinos opened. He went on to list a number of tragic criminal cases stemming from the newly available gambling—from the manager of a pizza restaurant who embezzled $45,000, to a U.S. Air Force sergeant who got hooked on slot machines and murdered a casino operator in an attempt to recover a few bad checks he had passed. Both men previously had spotless criminal records.[8]

Bloomberg currently serves as commissioner of the Bureau of Administration, which handles purchasing for South Dakota state offices. He said the state has become thoroughly dependent on gambling revenues. "To be honest with you, if we didn't have that money, we'd be hurting. We wouldn't be able to make it," he said. "The general attitude is, plug your nose and live with it."

Gambling opponents maintain the video lottery machines are the most pernicious and addictive form of gambling in the state. Their ubiquity turns the machines into a form of "convenience gambling" and not "destination gambling," meaning they rely on locally based gamblers instead of tourists. Joy and other opponents have tried to get rid of the machines through three statewide voter referendums from 1992 to 2006. (Plus, voters got their say a fourth time in 1994 after the State Supreme Court scrapped the video lottery on constitutional grounds, prompting legislators to sponsor a referendum to reinstitute it.) Each time there were more votes to keep the machines than to get rid of them, though twice machine supporters won by thin margins. Video lottery opponents note that voters knew taxes would be raised as a result of video lottery going away, and yet still twice almost decided voluntarily to do so.

Republican State Senate majority leader Dave Knudson and his wife De Knudson, a former member of the Sioux Falls City Council, have long been opponents of the video lottery. "There are just so many negatives to it," Dave Knudson said in an interview. They include the addiction spurred by the machines, he said; the aesthetic degradation of countless streets now littered with neon "casino" signs anywhere there are a few machines; and the exploitative "add-on" industries that have arrived with the gambling, including payday loan stores and pawnshops. But he doubts there will be another effort to ban the machines or to reduce gambling of any kind in the state, any time soon. "Nobody dreamed that it would be as big a business as it's turned into," he said. "It's a shame. It just junks up your cities."

Over the last two decades, states around the country have been turning toward the South Dakota model of legalized gambling—inundation—in increasing numbers. The main reason for the push is clear: gambling revenues shore up budget deficits, allow for reduced taxes, and pay for important programs from public works to public education. Collectively, these budget shortfalls are mammoth. By the end of fiscal year 2010, state governments around the nation were looking at an expected $127 billion fiscal hole.[9] Despite adverse consequences in the form of higher addiction rates and increased social costs, gambling repeatedly has been deemed by state-level politicians to be in the public interest. The recession of the late 2000s only aided their efforts. Desperate officials are turning to gambling as an economic cure-all. They see no other form of revenue generation as tempting or as politically feasible. And though voters are still generally wary of gambling—the closer the proposed casino is to their home, the more wary of it they are—the relentless efforts of gambling supporters are beginning to wear them down.

Proponents know they have time and money on their side. When gambling expansion proposals get shot down—as voters have been doing slightly more than half the time over the last several years—advocates simply have to reintroduce the idea sometime before the next election. Much better funded than their opponents, they can afford to lose several battles in a row if necessary. They need to win just once. Because when they win, it's for the long haul. Expansion supporters know that when gambling becomes legalized, it's virtually impossible to get rid of, in significant part because of voters' fears of increased taxes or reduced government services. The taste of the proceeds they believe are "painless" only spurs more efforts to expand.

This cycle is aided by states' sense of competition with one another. It's a phenomenon that has reached epidemic proportions in the Northeast, as even the possibility of increased gambling in some states has caused acute envy among their neighbors anxious to regain what they consider rightly to be theirs: the gambling losses of their own residents. New Jersey has casinos but wants legalized sports betting, too. Pennsylvania, Delaware, and Maryland throw themselves into the mix with slots parlors or "racinos"—racetracks flush with slot machines—which Pennsylvania and Delaware have now turned into something closer to full-fledged casinos with table games. Meanwhile, Connecticut's two mammoth and hugely profitable Indian casinos, Foxwoods Resort Casino and Mohegan Sun, have benefited from gamblers who live in neighboring states. This has spurred officials in New York, Rhode Island, Massachusetts, New Hampshire, and Maine to fast-track their own casino proposals. The list goes on, and the Northeast is just the most glaring example of these regional one-upmanship contests.

This trend has been in existence since the early 1990s, but it picked up significant steam when the economic downturn took hold in 2008. The most candid pro-gambling politicians haven't been reluctant to explain their reasoning. In 1993, then-Philadelphia Mayor Ed Rendell lobbied for casino riverboats. He said he believed that by 2000, most urban areas would have some form of gambling. Whatever harm Philadelphia's riverboat gamblers might face is harm they'd be facing if the boats didn't exist, he suggested. "If people are going to gamble away their paychecks, better they do it here than in Atlantic City," he said.[10]

Yet repeated studies have shown that newly legalized gambling opportunities create new gamblers. It doesn't simply siphon off those who gamble at other legal venues or who gamble illegally. People who didn't gamble before begin to do so. A small subset of those folks gets hooked. What's more, the overall gambling market—including legal and illegal wagering—increases. The U.S. Justice Department among others has found that as legalized gambling grows, the amount of illegal gambling grows right along with it. Criminals, including in some cases organized crime syndicates, take advantage of new gambling markets by offering gamblers different types of competition, as well as credit and loans at usurious rates.

None of this is to mention what is arguably the main downside to legalizing gambling: the increased social costs the whole community pays for, including everything from escalated gambling-related crime to unemployment, bankruptcies, divorces, illnesses, and ultimately, suicides. Numerous studies have been conducted determining the average social costs borne by problem and pathological gamblers. One of the most comprehensive is by Baylor University economist Earl Grinols in his 2004 book *Gambling in America: Costs and Benefits*. Grinols found that addicted gamblers cost the United States between $32.4 billion and $53.8 billion per year, or, on average, $274 per adult. That's about 40 percent of what drug abusers cost the country. (The National Council on Problem Gambling estimates that total social costs reach a more modest $6.7 billion per year. Regardless of the actual number, the council believes that state and nonprofit services to prevent and treat problem gamblers save at least $2 for every dollar spent.)

At the same time, the growing dependence on gambling revenue is distorting how states are governed. According to one study a few years ago, seventeen states generated more than 5 percent of their revenues from commercial casinos, racinos, and lotteries.[11] "Absolutely, we're addicted to gambling dollars," Iowa state representative Kraig Paulsen, an expansion opponent, said in early 2010. He noted that his state currently receives about $300 million a year from the industry. "The current budget couldn't be close to being balanced without that money."[12]

Expansion proponents are often quick to note their concern about gamblers who develop problems because of the new casinos, lotteries, or racinos they're promoting. That's why these officials usually agree to set aside a small portion of the profits for problem gambling prevention, public awareness, and treatment programs. It shouldn't take a skeptic to conclude this is what they're actually saying: "We know we are willfully creating a new subclass of addicts in our community. But we promise we'll at least try to fix them and mitigate the damage."

Gambling, since before America's declared independence, has for long stretches played an important role in how our local governments have raised revenue. This in part has depended on gambling's status—its level of general acceptance as a morally appropriate activity. Though it may be difficult to imagine in our current gambling-glutted environment, there also have been a few points in our history when prohibition forces decimated what by then were vibrant periods of lotteries, riverboat gambling, and small private casinos—only to see those prohibitions eroded through more and more legalized gambling. This is what gambling historian and legal expert I. Nelson Rose refers to as "our cycles of complete prohibition to complete permissiveness and back again."[13] He calls these periods America's three "waves" of gambling.

State lotteries were prevalent in the colonial period, but other forms of gambling—dice, decks of cards, gambling tables—were outlawed, even in private homes. As colonial America grew, and then after America broke free from Great Britain, lotteries funded everything from roads and bridges to the capital projects of prominent universities, including Columbia University and the University of North Carolina.[14] In the early 1800s, lotteries of all sorts, including privately run ventures, continued to prosper. Though private operators paid licensing fees to the state, there usually was little or no government oversight. This led to widespread corruption. Some operators claimed they hadn't sold enough tickets to pay winners. In the worst cases, money was collected, but the drawings were never even held. The scandals, and a growing sense of moral revulsion, prompted states to ban lotteries in their constitutions and caused the federal government likewise to pass anti-lottery statutes. By 1862, only two states had not banned lotteries altogether, Kentucky and Missouri.

The country's second gambling wave began as the Civil War ended and Reconstruction began. Many southern states reopened licensed lotteries as a way to raise revenue. Some, including Louisiana's, made much of their profits through sales to northern state residents. Gambling also thrived in Wild West casinos during this period, though there were laws on many of the local government's books outlawing the games. But as the nineteenth century drew to a close, a second round of lottery scandals, as well as a growing sense from Western political leaders that the region's new states shouldn't be brought into existence as gambling meccas, effectively shut down gambling throughout the country, again. By 1895, all state lotteries had ended, and within another fifteen years, only Kentucky and Maryland had maintained legalized horse race betting. This effectively meant a second prohibition had begun.

The nation's third main period of legalized gambling began during the Great Depression—and as the country suffers through its biggest recession since then, gambling remains, flourishing. Nevada, which had banned gambling in 1909, legalized it again in 1931. Over the course of that decade, more than twenty states opened horse tracks with pari-mutuel betting. Bingo halls, usually played for charity, were opened in the 1940s and 1950s. And after about seventy years without them, New Hampshire opened the country's first modern-era state lottery in 1964.

This ongoing third gambling wave picked up considerable steam in the late 1980s, when the U.S. Supreme Court and then Congress paved the way for full-fledged casinos on Indian reservations. By 1996, half of the states allowed casinos of various forms, including Indian and commercial-owned, on land and riverboat. Since then, the momentum for more gambling has increased. And just in case there was a threat of a slowdown, the recession cemented the notion—for the time being, anyway—of legalized gambling as an accepted state revenue-builder and entertainment option.

The timing of these gambling revivals was no accident. Bad times have always spurred legalized gambling. Citizens, not to mention their elected representatives, have repeatedly been willing to fund tax cuts and prop up sagging state governments by increasing revenues from legalized gambling. In 1978, Californians passed Proposition 13, sharply reducing property taxes. Six years later, the revenue loss was offset by newly legalized lotteries. "In each of these periods, state governments faced great difficulty in raising revenue through traditional means of taxation, and resorted to legalizing various forms of gambling to generate revenue by tapping the lucre from a previously banned product," Raymond Sauer, a Clemson University economics professor, said in a 2010 *New York Times* column.[15]

Of course, the cycles of gambling legalization have to do with more than economics. Shifting moral perceptions of gambling and its place in society—similar to changing ideas about alcohol and drugs—also have played a big role. "The anti-gambling prohibitions epitomize the traditional approach taken by American laws. These laws are not only designed to protect people from themselves. They are part of a greater moral framework, designed by policy makers as a reflection of an imagined ideal society," writes Rose. Increased legalization leads to a greater sense of permissiveness, he says: "The Victorian morality that says *nothing is permitted* is replaced by the belief that *everything is permitted, so long as you do not hurt another person.* And gambling is the least harmful of the victimless crimes."[16]

But here's the thing. It's not just opponents who believe that gambling produces many types of victims, from the addicts to those around them and even whole communities, which pick up the tab for problem gamblers' social costs. Recent national surveys send mixed signals regarding how Americans view gambling and whether they want it to be part of their lives or in their neighborhoods.

According to a 2010 Gallup poll of about one thousand American adults, 61 percent of those polled found gambling to be "morally acceptable" behavior; 34 percent viewed it as "morally wrong."[17] The overall percentage of those who view gambling as morally acceptable has remained steady since 2003. The same is true for the slightly higher percentage of American adults—about two out of three—who told Gallup in 2007 and 2003 that they've gambled at least once in the previous twelve months. This hasn't come without a cost. In the 2003 survey, 6 percent of those questioned said they gambled more than they should. Likewise, 6 percent said gambling had been the source of problems in their families.[18]

According to other major national surveys, a growing number are viewing gambling with some alarm. A 2006 Pew Research Center report found that 70 percent of Americans believed that legalized gambling encouraged people to gamble more than they can afford. That's appreciably higher than the 62 percent who answered yes to the same question in 1989. "The negative turn in attitudes toward gambling appears to be driven by concerns that people are gambling too much rather than by any revival of the once common view that gambling is immoral," the 2006 report concluded.[19]

Despite voters and politicians agreeing to ever-more legalized gambling, casinos appear to be among the least popular of many types of neighborhood developments. In a 2010 poll conducted by the Saint Consulting Group, 72 percent of the Americans polled said they were against a casino being built in their community.[20] Of the fourteen types of proposed developments mentioned, including a Walmart, a hospital, and a grocery store, only landfills were less popular. (In the most recent Saint poll taken in Canada, casinos took the top spot, proving to be even less popular as a possible neighborhood development than landfills.) In the American survey, 5 percent fewer respondents objected to a casino being built in Saint's 2010 poll than in 2009. But this was the case with most other large developments as well. "Saint Index 2010 results suggest the prolonged economic downturn is undermining America's Not In My Back Yard (NIMBY) attitude, but interviews also found resistance to development persists when Americans look at their own community," the poll's authors wrote.[21]

This NIMBY attitude extends to some surprising people. In an October 2006 debate in Cleveland with the antigambling activist Tom Grey, Frank Fahrenkopf Jr.—president and CEO of the American Gaming Association, the powerful trade group for the commercial casino industry—conceded that casinos were not appropriate for every neighborhood. Meaning, specifically, his own upscale Washington, D.C., suburb.

"The people have the right to go to the ballot box and determine what they want the quality of life to be in their own area," Fahrenkopf said in a video clip of the debate found on two different recordings posted on YouTube.com.[22] "Now, if someone were to come along and tell me that they were going to put a casino in McLean, Virginia, where I live, I would probably work very, very hard against it. I just don't . . . What's the old saying, NIMBY, not in my backyard. Now, I may be in favor of gaming, but I just don't want it located in a particular area."

In 2009 and 2010, state legislators and their gambling industry allies have been pushing gambling to be legalized in an unprecedented number of backyards. According to the National Conference of State Legislatures' annual online tally of state developments regarding gambling,[23] in addition to my own reporting, in 2009, twenty-four states sought to expand gambling in some fashion. In 2010, that number shot up to thirty-five states. Over the two-year period, a whopping thirty-seven states, at least, sought to expand gambling, including one state, Hawaii, which debated whether to introduce legalized gambling for the first time.

Following is a brief synopsis of these thirty-seven state efforts, listed alphabetically by state, during the two-year period. This is not a comprehensive or complete summary of each state's actions. Rather, view it as a snapshot. It should be noted that in the cases where a final vote was taken, it appears that about as many expansion efforts failed as passed. But gambling historians note that this failure rate used to be much higher. In other words, voters are approving gambling at a higher rate than they did one or two decades ago. In the end, I would submit an equally important trend is the increasing number of expansion proposals being put on the table. Taken as a whole, it's easy to conclude there is a legalized gambling avalanche in progress in America.

In Alabama, a proposal that would have regulated electronic bingo machines and authorized fourteen locations in the state for their operation failed in the state senate. Arizona allowed charitable organizations to sell instant games, known as scratch tickets, issued by its state lottery. Racetrack owners in the state also pushed for legislation for slot machines to be added to their tracks to turn them into racinos. Arkansas became the forty-third state to legalize a lottery. Soon after, they expanded it by joining the Powerball multistate lottery and by placing lottery ticket vending machines at high-volume retail stores throughout the state.

California state lawmakers passed a bill to the governor's office in 2010 that would allow "exchange wagering" at the state's horse race-tracks. In essence, this would permit bettors to wager against one another, meaning gamblers could place bets that a horse will lose. In Colorado, gambling expansions approved by voters, including increased betting limits, expanded casino hours, and the addition of table games, took effect in 2009. The following year, after proposals for keno and a new racino failed, a new proposal was put forth that would allow for video lottery terminals, in the hopes that they would raise $100 million per year for the state lottery. Connecticut's governor proposed introducing keno in her state-of-the-state speech. She estimated the game would raise $60 million a year. Also, a bill was put forth to expand simulcast betting of horse and other races.

In Delaware, the legislature approved legalized sports betting (though court rulings subsequently limited the state's sports betting plans) and allowed casinos to add table games such as blackjack and poker. Florida approved a new compact with the Seminole Indians that will legalize some table games at five tribal casino sites for five years. It also gave the tribe the rights to operate Vegas-style slot machines at all of its seven casinos for twenty years. The state also allowed the poker rooms in Indian casinos and attached to dog and horse race facilities and jai alai frontons to increase their betting limits and hours of operation. In Georgia, a proposal at the state legislature failed that would have given cities and counties the authority to approve horse racing, dog racing, casinos, or any combination of the three.

Hawaii legislators sponsored two bills to open a casino— measures, had they passed, that would have allowed legalized gambling on the islands for the first time. By early 2010, both bills had failed. Illinois was chock-full of activity. The state approved a measure allowing video poker machines in bars, restaurants, and social clubs. The legislation could allow up to forty-five thousand machines in the state. To stem declining revenues at riverboat casinos, a measure was put forth to allow free alcoholic drinks so gamblers would play and lose more. There also was a bill to allow racetracks to create racinos, and yet another 2010 measure that would financially penalize cities that ban video gambling operations. In Indiana, a proposal failed that would have allowed for the creation of land-based casinos.

In Iowa, the state's Racing and Gaming Commission approved a state license for a $120-million casino in a county near the South Dakota and Minnesota state borders. But further efforts in Iowa to legalize sports betting and to approve casinos at four additional locations failed. In Kansas, a measure failed that would have allowed the Wichita Greyhound Park to become a racino by adding up to twenty-two hundred slot machines. Meanwhile, a casino opened in Dodge City, and another, at the Kansas City Raceway, is slated to be finished in 2012. The Kentucky legislature failed to pass a racino proposal in 2010, as it did in each of the previous two years.

Louisiana lawmakers put forth a bill that would create a tax district to fund an economic development project next to the Hollywood Casino in Baton Rouge. In Maine, legislation to allow a casino was postponed by the legislature, but an initiative to allow the casino was set to go before voters statewide in November of 2010. Similar efforts were rejected by the legislature in 2009, and by voters the year before. Maryland opened its first slot machine parlor in 2010, and another was set to open by the end of the year.

In Massachusetts, a 2010 bill that would have allowed for three resort-style casinos and two additional slot machine parlors attached to racetracks was sent back to the state legislature by Governor Deval Patrick. Though he supports the casinos, Patrick is against the idea of the slot parlors, especially if they're connected to racetracks. In

Michigan, a ballot signature campaign was undertaken that would expand casino gambling to seven new locations. Minnesota lawmakers weighed whether to allow their racetracks to become racinos.

A bill to create a state lottery failed in Mississippi in 2010. In Missouri, state officials weighed whether to expand bingo hall playing hours, and in a separate matter, whether to issue a new casino license, bringing the total number of casinos in the state to thirteen. A bill to allow Nebraska's five racetracks to become racinos failed in 2010. But a bill allowing a new racetrack was passed.

In Nevada, state legislators unsuccessfully pushed for the creation of a state lottery in 2009. That was the twenty-seventh failed attempt for a lottery in Nevada since 1975. A New Hampshire bill to create racinos by adding seventeen thousand slot machines or video lottery machines and table games at a total of six greyhound and harness racetracks failed. The governor suggested that instead, the state consider legalizing online gambling sites. In New Jersey, because of plummeting casino revenues and consistently high crime rates, Governor Chris Christie in 2010 proposed that the state take over an array of functions from Atlantic City and other local bodies. This would put the state in charge of reducing crime, spurring development, and promoting the area to tourists. Christie also issued an executive order to create a commission to study sports betting. And a bill that would have granted licenses to Atlantic City casinos for online gambling failed.

In New York, state lottery officials moved forward with their plans to turn Aqueduct Racetrack in Queens into a racino. It's expected to feature about forty-five hundred slot machines. New Mexico's Gaming Control Board was set in 2010 to decide whether a proposed racino would keep its license. Meanwhile, North Carolina tribal and state officials explored whether to expand casino gambling to include live card games. Also, legislation was introduced to legalize electronic video gaming.

Ohio voters in 2009 authorized the development of four casinos, each with up to five thousand slot machines. Another measure was in play that, if passed, would mandate the Ohio lottery to operate video lottery terminals at the state's horse racetracks. Pennsylvania's gaming control board allowed five casinos to operate up to 250 table games each, and several of these newly bulked-up racinos and slot parlors began operating in 2010. However, a measure to introduce video poker machines into the state's bars and restaurants stalled. In Rhode Island, legislators proposed a bill allowing up to two new casinos.

In South Dakota, as mentioned earlier in the chapter, an Indian tribe and some local residents are proposing a new casino in or near Sioux Falls. In Texas, legislators allied with the horse and greyhound racing industries are considering introducing legislation to allow racetracks to have video lottery terminals. In 2010, the Washington State Gambling Commission filed a proposal to create a pilot program to allow $100 wagers in Texas Hold'em poker games in state-licensed card rooms that qualify. Finally, in Wyoming, a bill to create a state lottery was defeated in 2009.

When looking to install a new casino or other gambling venue, proponents tout several benefits, but a few usually rise to the top: jobs, economic growth, and increased/improved entertainment options. All three arguments appear to have at least some merit.

In 1998, researcher Adam Rose examined one hundred studies that had been written about the economic benefits and costs of casinos. His forty-seven-page paper, prepared for the National Gambling Impact Study Commission, didn't study the social costs of gambling (aside from a brief look at increased crime), which many other researchers have concluded is vitally important while weighing the overall impact of new gambling on communities. But he did look at several other important economic gauges regarding how casinos affect local governments, and his conclusions were mostly positive.

Casino jobs have proven beneficial to several areas of the country—including Indian reservations, the rural South, and inner cities—places where "immediate employment" is otherwise impossible to come by, Rose found. Gambling taxes typically more than pay for what otherwise would be spent on road improvements and fire and police department funding. And claims that local businesses such as restaurants and entertainment outlets become "cannibalized" by new casinos are "grossly exaggerated," he concluded.[24]

The real benefit from gambling legalization is a notion called "consumer surplus," said Bill Eadington, an economist who is director of the Institute for the Study of Gambling and Commercial Gaming at the University of Nevada, Reno, in an interview. Eadington has studied gambling trends for decades, written scores of papers on the topic, and is among the most widely quoted experts in the field. Consumer surplus, he said, is the satisfaction that customers gain from the activity. From a more narrow economics framework, such a surplus can be felt when increased competition causes lower prices. This pertains to gambling when two casinos are competing and one offers gambling consumers better payouts, for example, or when a casino boasts restaurants that, because of competition with local eateries, offer lower prices.

Eadington was quoted in a mid-2010 newspaper story saying that gambling expansion efforts have reached a "tipping point."[25] Meaning, among voters and state legislators, the tide seems to have turned in favor of gambling proponents. Until 2007 and 2008, there was reluctance to expand gambling in some states worried about social costs, he's suggested, but that is no longer the case. "It has become so prevalent," he told me, "that it's no longer a question of whether to legalize, but where."

Eadington said state leaders believe "we want job creation, we want development, and we don't want our citizens crossing state lines to gamble." But he noted that new gambling developments are "a very mixed bag" for communities. There are valid aesthetic concerns, he said, and gambling can understandably be seen as a "low road" option both for entertainment and for raising state revenues. Plus, he said, "If you're a non-gambler, you're probably healthier than if you're a gambler."

It's worth noting that Eadington's work is funded in part through his position as the Philip G. Satre Chair in Gaming Studies at the university. Satre was CEO of casino giant Harrah's Entertainment for about a decade (in November 2010, Harrah's changed its name to Caesars Entertainment) and currently serves on the board of directors of the country's largest slot machine manufacturer, International Game Technology. The chair's endowment is in large part funded by the gambling industry. In 2004, Harrah's committed $1 million to the Satre Chair endowment at the university, and several other gambling businesses also made donations. From 2005 to 2010, about $120,000 per year has been forwarded from the endowment to the institute, Eadington said. Another nationally known gambling researcher, John Warren Kindt, who has been consistently critical of the industry, has called Eadington "a well-known apologist for the gambling industry."[26] Eadington emphatically denied that his institute's funding has influenced his research or that he's ever written a paper or made a public comment with the purpose of supporting a gambling legalization effort.

Eadington is not the only researcher of gambling's economic effects who's been criticized for his industry-funding ties. Clyde Barrow is a tenured professor at the University of Massachusetts, Dartmouth. According to a *Boston Globe* article, he "has become the undisputed king of academic research on gambling trends in New England."[27] His studies have been touted by Governor Patrick in Massachusetts, among other gambling supporters, as evidence that casinos are a wise economic bet for their state. Barrow has also caught flack a couple of times because his research, directly and indirectly, has been funded by gambling industry sources. Like Eadington, he has strenuously denied that his research has been tainted in any way because of it. He's noted that his work is peer-reviewed by other academics and published in scholarly journals. In 2010, Barrow and a colleague published a study defending the substance of his previous work, noting that policy research on the issue of expanded gambling "is invariably politicized by its release into a highly charged and polarized political environment. . . . Applied policy research may be scientifically valid and empirically accurate, but that does not mean that such information is politically neutral in its policy implications or practical impact."[28]

A couple of states away, former Philadelphia mayor and now outgoing Democratic governor Ed Rendell has in his two terms in Harrisburg become one of the most active pro-gambling governors in the country. Between the sixty-one thousand slot machines he successfully sought in 2004, to the table games he legalized six years later, to the video poker machines he hoped would be placed in bars and restaurants throughout the state even more recently, it's fair to say gambling will be a big part of his political legacy. "He's got to be the most gung ho gambling proponent that I've known," said Dan Hajdo, a spokesman with Casino-Free Philadelphia.

Rendell won election in 2002 by making big promises to lower taxes and bring new business to the state. But once in office, he encountered more obstacles than he thought he might—and found legalized gambling as the answer. In his second major effort to pass a gambling bill, over the July Fourth weekend in 2004, Rendell, backed by what an opponent called "every lobbyist in Harrisburg," according to one media account,[29] persuaded lawmakers in both chambers to jam the measure through in speedy fashion. In the "darkest hours" of July 4th, "the colossal bill passed with no public scrutiny, no hearings, and no input from citizens."

In an interview, Rendell sounded at turns both combative and reflective. He emphasized that Pennsylvania was receiving $1 billion per year in revenues from gamblers who were hopping across state lines to spend the money before he legalized slot machines and table games. "We're surrounded!" he said, by states with established or burgeoning gambling scenes. So why on earth should he be missing out on the jobs created and the funds to lower property taxes for his residents? Legalized gambling has created nine thousand direct jobs and another fifteen thousand indirect jobs, he said, referring to those in related industries created because of the new gambling businesses.

Rendell, who is term-limited out of office in January 2011, said he has no regrets about his efforts to thrust gambling into the state. He called it a "grand-slam home run" and a "win-win" for the taxpayers and the gamblers who now don't need to drive as far to hit the slots or play some blackjack. "I'm at peace with everything I've done as governor. This is a part of what I've done," he said. He bristled when asked whether the state, by bolstering its efforts to fund problem gambling treatment, was in effect recognizing it had a role in helping create problem gamblers. He referred to a figure from the Pennsylvania Gaming Control Board that only 144 people had engaged in services through the state's Compulsive Gambling Treatment Fund since gambling was expanded throughout the state. "One hundred and forty-four in three years? Give me a break," he said. In a June 2010 letter from the chair of the Pennsylvania Gaming Control Board to the *Philadelphia Inquirer*, the official noted that figure and concluded that, "As to the evils of addiction cited by the *Inquirer*, the Commonwealth has not witnessed an onslaught of addicted gamblers seeking treatment."[30]

In fact, other, arguably more convincing data show there has been a clear and significant rise in the last three years among gamblers in Pennsylvania who have become so distressed that they've reached out for help. According to Jim Pappas, executive director of the Council on Compulsive Gambling of Pennsylvania, there are four toll-free telephone numbers listed in casinos and elsewhere for gamblers seeking help. In February 2007, those lines received a combined nine hundred calls. By late 2010, when we spoke, the number had doubled to eighteen hundred calls per month. Of those, he said fifty to sixty people are referred monthly for treatment, a number that's also risen. He added that while the state program is beneficial, it services only a portion of the problem gamblers in Pennsylvania who seek treatment.

A side note to this story sheds light on exactly what information Rendell's administration was looking for as it geared up for its 2004 expansion fight—and what facts it didn't care to know.

In 2003, a citizens group asked William N. Thompson, a veteran gambling researcher out of the University of Nevada, Las Vegas, to study whether thirty thousand new slot machines located in up to fourteen new casinos would be in the public interest, and then to present his findings to the finance committees of the Pennsylvania General Assembly. He estimated where the players would come from and where the profits would go. He found that $450 million would leave the state immediately to pay for the machines, and that the casino profits would go to the owners, many of whom were based out of state. And none of this was to take into account the social costs that would result. He concluded that thirty thousand machines would result in a net loss of several hundred million dollars a year for the state, despite the considerable amount in taxes the state would reap.

A few weeks later, Thompson got a call from Rendell's office. They had read his report and wanted him to conduct more research. He thought the governor wanted to know more about the risks the state was taking by installing new casinos. That wasn't it. "A staff member soon straightened me out," he wrote in the 2010 *Villanova Sports and Entertainment Law Journal*.[31] Instead, Rendell wanted more information on how much money slot machines made in various spots around the United States—and how much in taxes his state could expect from a new, slightly higher proposal of thirty-five thousand machines. Specifically, they wanted to know if thirty-five thousand machines could result in taxes of $1 billion per year for the state. Thompson found that with a 33 percent tax rate, the state could expect to win between $930 million and $1.2 billion per year as its tax share.

"The only thing the governor's office wanted to know about was taxes, not the public interest," wrote Thompson, referring to an overall look at the effect of the proposed slots. "A month or so later, I was surprised when the governor's office released a statement revising their proposal. They now wanted the state to authorize *sixty thousand* machines. I guess they really liked my report."

The influx of lobbyists to Pennsylvania's capital to back Rendell's gambling bill wasn't unique. In Grinols's *Gambling in America,* as well as in Robert Goodman's path-breaking 1995 book *The Luck Business: The Devastating Consequences and Broken Promises of America's Gambling Explosion,* they list several instances in which the gambling industry—knowing that a hefty investment in lobbying was worth the expenditure even with a strong risk of losing— has flooded lots of state capitals over the years. Grinols writes that, according to a report from Kindt, casino proponents in Richmond, Virginia, hired no fewer than four dozen lobbyists in 1995, not just to promote a riverboat gambling bill but also, in effect, to rig the game in their favor. They hired lobbyists from "virtually every lobbying firm in the capital to prevent anti-gambling groups from hiring lobbyists to compete."[32]

The knock on Grinols and Kindt, a professor of business and legal policy at the University of Illinois, from the gambling industry and a few other observers is that they draw conclusions first and then collect data to support those conclusions, which typically take a dim view of the gambling industry. Both have denied the allegation.

And both have strong academic backgrounds. Grinols, for example, has taught at Cornell University and the University of Chicago and served as a senior economist for the Council of Economic Advisers.

Ultimately, the evidence that Grinols, Kindt, and Goodman collectively have documented over the years regarding how the costs of legalized gambling outweigh its economic and social benefits holds considerable weight.

Grinols and Kindt have referred to one of the benchmark economics-based explanations as to why legalized gambling is not a healthy long-term policy, written by Paul Samuelson, the first American to win the Nobel Prize in Economics. In his book called *Economics: An Introductory Analysis,* Samuelson found that there is a "substantial" economic case to be made against gambling. It involves *"sterile transfers of money* between individuals, creating no new value," he wrote. "While creating no value, gambling does nevertheless absorb time and resources. When pursued beyond the limits of recreation, where the main purpose after all is to 'kill' time, gambling subtracts from the national income."[33]

According to Grinols's calculations, the costs of problem and pathological gambling—which include the social costs mentioned above as well as lost productivity, lost work time, and unemployment—outweigh the combined benefits of legalized gambling by a significant margin. "The long-term cost-to-benefit ratio from introducing casinos to a region that did not have them previously is greater than 3:1. As a device for raising taxes, casinos are more socially costly than a conventional tax," Grinols writes.[34]

The tens of billions of dollars spent per year on legalized gambling would boost the economy if used more efficiently, Kindt has noted. "That's lost consumer activity that's not buying food, clothing, cars, refrigerators, and so on," he said.[35]

In *The Luck Business,* Goodman notes that during the expansion mini-wave of the early 1990s, most of the casinos were built in declining communities in states such as Mississippi, Indiana, and Louisiana and failed to replicate the Las Vegas model so many politicians dreamed of, in which gamblers would come as tourists, lose money, and then leave. These expansion efforts "dramatically transformed most of America's 1990s gambling economy into what many people in the gambling industry began to call 'convenience gambling'—casino and electronic gambling machine operations in bars, convenience stores, and racetracks, which would rely on a community's local residents for most of their customers," Goodman wrote. Rather than adding new revenues, development, and jobs, "it simply reshuffles what exists in these communities."[36]

A more recent survey backed the notion that economic growth, as reflected by per capita income, does not rise over the long haul when a state legalizes gambling. The study, by economists Douglas M. Walker and John D. Jackson, studied data from the eleven states that had commercial casinos during the years 1991 to 2005. An earlier study on the same topic from the same researchers found that from 1991 to 1996, there was a positive correlation; per capita income did rise as a result of casinos. According to their more recent 2007 study, however, they suggest one theory for the thinning positive effect is that the effects of expansion on "the average state" diminish over time, possibly because of competition from casinos in neighboring states or online gambling. "Adopting casino gambling appears to at first provide a boost to the economy, but that boost appears to be relatively short-lived," they found.[37] Casinos might well positively impact economic growth in states such as Nevada and New Jersey. But "the average state should not expect any long-term growth effects from legalizing casino gambling," they concluded.

Whether legalizing gambling is a smart economic move for states, it raises big concerns as social policy, experts say. Robert Ward, deputy director of the Nelson A. Rockefeller Institute of Government, noted how states freely express concerns about citizens engaging in other habits widely considered to be unhealthy and offer programs to reduce the activity. With gambling, it's often the opposite. "It's ironic that states are using tax policy to reduce cigarette smoking and discourage unhealthy eating, at the same time they are promoting more gambling and thus more social pathology," said Ward in an e-mailed response to questions. "It's very hard to conclude that every marginal increase in state-sanctioned gambling pulls in someone who otherwise would be involved in illegal gambling. In other words, the states almost certainly are creating new gamblers—and a certain number of those folks are finding out first-hand what addiction is all about."

At the new slot parlors and racinos Governor Rendell of Pennsylvania fought for, the new gamblers are mostly local—and many are exhibiting symptoms that could only reflect an addiction. At Parx Racing and Casino just outside Philadelphia, the revenue from their thirty-five hundred slot machines and fifty-seven table games comes almost exclusively from local "low rollers," casino president Dave Jonas said at the Pennsylvania Gaming Congress in early 2010, most of whom live within twenty miles of the facility. Often, they show up 150 to 200 times per year to gamble, and usually lose, small amounts. "We underestimated significantly how many trips our customers were going to make," he said.[38]

During the unseasonably hot summer months of 2010, seven different customers left thirteen children, including a fifteen-month-old, unattended in their cars so they could run in and feed the slots for a while or play some roulette.[39] In September, several state and local politicians, a police director, and casino executives held a news conference. They said enough was enough: tough action was needed. They proposed making a felony out of stranding children in vacant cars to gamble. Three hours after the press event ended, a man shut his twelve-year-old grandson in an SUV for a half hour without keys, air-conditioning, or water, to play Parx's slot machines. It was 94 degrees outside.

The good news is that the man was up $100 when police nabbed him.

CHAPTER 2

Welcome to Las Vegas, Problem Gambling Capital of the World

Walk into a Las Vegas casino, or any of the almost countless bars, groceries, and retailers throughout the region with video poker machines, and there is a good chance you will see a rack of glossy pamphlets showing an orange sun setting over a black ocean. The words WHEN THE FUN STOPS are stenciled above the image.

Every eighteen to twenty-four months, the Nevada Council on Problem Gambling prints a 200,000-copy run of its brochure. For more than a decade, the council has sold the brochures in order to help satisfy Nevada Gaming Commission regulations that require every licensed gambling outlet in the state to provide information on the nature and symptoms of problem gambling in "conspicuous places," including ATMs and casino cages.

Some casino companies produce their own materials. But several others, including MGM Mirage and Station Casinos, have used the council's brochures for years (MGM Mirage changed its name to MGM Resorts International in June 2010). The council distributes the remainder to local seniors facilities, community centers, and schools as part of its efforts to raise awareness about the dangers of gambling. Inside, the pamphlet provides a description of problem gambling, a listing of warning signs, and a toll-free number to call for help.

The catch phrase "When the Fun Stops" was devised by Howie C., who has contributed more than anyone over the last four decades to support problem gamblers in Las Vegas—and arguably the country. "One of things I'm most proud of is, you know the 'When the Fun Stops' brochures that are all around the state? That was my idea," he said. "I coined that phrase. The thing I'm happy about is that they have to be there, by state law. They have to be everywhere there are machines."

Howie—who asked that he not be identified by his full last name given his thirty-seven years in Gamblers Anonymous—is a small, trim man with a gray and white goatee that points off of an angular face. At seventy-one, he is clear-spoken and has a sharp recollection of recent and decades-old events in his life. We spoke over a late breakfast at a Las Vegas diner.

The story of Howie's descent into addiction is not exceptional. What is extraordinary is the story of how in the early years, beginning with his first GA meeting, he nearly single-handedly built the infrastructure to aid problem gamblers in Las Vegas, and then, part of the rest of the United States. When I mentioned to a friend of mine from GA in Seattle that I was moving to Las Vegas, he urged me to look Howie up.

"He's a legend," he said.

Howie first reached his gambling limit in 1971, six years after moving his family from Los Angeles to Las Vegas to become a professional gambler. Quickly realizing that he would not be successful in his new choice of profession, he found a career in the casino business, like many Vegas gamblers. Howie spun so out of control that he contemplated suicide because of his gambling, so he searched for a Gamblers Anonymous meeting in Las Vegas. Unable to find any GA presence in the nation's gambling capital, he took his family on vacation to San Diego and attended his first GA meeting there.

It was a revelation to be able to tell his story to others who had undergone similar traumas and to hear their stories. The other gamblers told him about the one small weekly meeting then held in Las Vegas and how to find it. He showed up the following Monday evening at a Methodist church just blocks away from the downtown casinos. Five people including Howie sat around a card table. But it was a different experience than the San Diego meeting. Only two of the five attendees spoke—by engaging in an hour-long argument—and a couple of the people actually were there to get gambling tips, not to talk about the destructiveness of their habit and their need to quit. It was like an alcoholic showing up to an AA meeting because he needed directions to the nearest bar.

Howie concluded that he needed to get involved and set up other weekly groups. In part, this was self-preservation: he had to attend, and therefore create, meetings closer to the beginning of the weekend, or there was a greater chance he'd slip and gamble. He quickly became the founding father of the GA movement in Las Vegas. For the first decade after he started with GA, he founded all of the meetings in Vegas. And he took on all the necessary roles to help the meetings grow: founder, meeting chair, secretary, public relations liaison. "Every position there is in GA, I did them all," he said. By 1981, he estimated that there were twenty-eight different weekly meetings in the region. He also helped start meetings in several western and southern states, and internationally, in England, Iceland, and Australia.

In time, Howie founded the Nevada Council on Problem Gambling, an offshoot of the National Council on Problem Gambling that educates state residents and procures funding for treatment programs and a toll-free help line. For more than two decades he also worked as a counselor with the Problem Gambling Center in Las Vegas, the leading gambling treatment facility in the state. He was, as he says, a man of many hats.

That changed on March 18, 2009. After thirty-seven years of

abstinence, Howie gambled. Soon after, he left GA and was fired from the Problem Gambling Center after being spotted placing a sports bet at a locals casino in north Las Vegas. Robert Hunter, the founder and clinical director of the center, said he received e-mails from recovering gamblers around the world distressed by Howie's return to a gambling life. He said he urged them to dwell on the notion that Howie might someday come back to the movement—and that regardless, the good he did could never be undone.

"He can't do anything that erases the lives he's touched," said Hunter. "He's helped more people than Albert Schweitzer."

There's a reason why Howie was easily able to spread his gambling abstinence gospel during his early days in Las Vegas, and why after decades in recovery, he found himself in a position to fall off the wagon quickly. It's the same reason why many Las Vegans have suffered devastating downward spirals after finding themselves caught in gambling's grip.

Las Vegas possesses unique qualities for a city—its casino culture is embedded into neighborhoods far beyond the tourist-centered Las Vegas Strip and into the rest of the Las Vegas Valley. In addition to the more than two dozen huge casino resorts on the Strip, there are more than twenty-five full-service casinos specifically designed to lure the "locals" trade as opposed to tourists, as well as the dozen casino/hotels in the city's older downtown district, which also in part cater to locally based gamblers.

This gambling mecca has become the nation's problem gambling capital. In the last several decades, gambling has been absorbed into every facet of life in Las Vegas, and the consequences have been dire. Local residents have found themselves hooked. In turn, this has helped lead to higher gambling-related social costs than anywhere else in the country.

As voters around the country are weighing whether to expand

gambling's reach, and as the notion that increased availability of gambling leads to more problem gamblers gains credibility, where better to test this theory than Las Vegas? Where better to show what could happen to other cities and towns if gambling was legalized to anywhere near the same extent?

The Las Vegas area's population has exploded over the last decade and residents are inundated with opportunities to gamble. There are 14,000 video poker and slot machines that chime day and night in Clark County, which includes Las Vegas and its suburbs, in more than 1,400 restaurants and bars and retailers of all types, from big-chain groceries and drug stores to 7-Elevens and Kmarts.[1] That is not counting the 1,150 machines at McCarran International Airport.[2] They are seemingly everywhere.

Upon arrival, new residents find the highest problem and pathological gambling rates in the country and more Gamblers Anonymous chapter meetings than in any other city—fourteen per day on average. There are an estimated 115,000 adult problem and pathological gamblers in Nevada—mostly clustered in and around Las Vegas. Their issues have become fixed parts of the region's communal landscape.

Partially due to this, Las Vegas and Nevada boast higher rates of crime, bankruptcy filings, home foreclosures, divorces, and suicides than anywhere else in the country.

It would not be fair or correct to conclude that the highest problem gambling rates in the country were the direct and sole cause of these problems. For example, authorities have noted that local police have been unable to grow as fast as the population, a contributing factor to the high rate of crime. There are other similar, valid, if partial, explanations for each of these indicators—including the notion, bolstered by studies on the region, that Las Vegas often attracts people inclined to contribute to these social ills.

Yet in survey after survey, it has become clear that increased problem gambling leads to increased social costs. In dollar terms, a study on the topic coauthored by prominent University of Nevada, Las Vegas (UNLV), researchers concluded that problem and pathological gambling among southern Nevada residents results in costs conservatively estimated to be between $301 million and $469 million per year. There can be little question that Las Vegas is a damaged community—and no doubt at all that the effects of gambling's immersion into its culture has played a significant role.

At first, after gambling was legalized in Nevada in 1931, the casinos of downtown Las Vegas were open to local gamblers but catered primarily to tourists. In the early 1940s, as casinos spread south on Las Vegas Boulevard to form what is now known as the Strip, several casino operators recognized the long-term profit potential of catering to a local crowd. "They tended to be welcoming of locals. It wasn't, 'Oh, jeez, it's the hicks from the sticks.' A lot of them felt this is the goose laying the golden egg—they wanted to be good neighbors," said Michael Green, a history professor at the College of Southern Nevada and coauthor of *Las Vegas: A Centennial History.*

The first Las Vegas casino that marketed directly to local residents was the Showboat, a couple of miles east of downtown on Boulder Highway, which opened in 1954. Originally, the casino, housed in a Mississippi riverboat complete with a paddlewheel and smokestacks, hoped to compete with the Strip and downtown casinos by drawing well-heeled out-of-towners. But the casino fared poorly, and five years after opening, new owners decided to redirect its efforts away from expensive entertainers and toward the local market, low rollers, and family tourist trade. To attract the locals, the casino offered a 49-cent breakfast special and built a twenty-four-lane bowling alley—the types of good value staples soon to appear at locals casinos across the region. The Showboat became a hit and began enjoying repeat local customers.[3] The Palace Station followed suit, opening just west of the Strip at Sahara Avenue, in 1976. Three years later, Sam's Town opened on the east side of town.

As of mid-2010, two large chains operated the bulk of the locals casinos in southern Nevada. Station Casinos, Inc., which owns ten full-service casino/hotels anywhere from one mile to about a dozen away from the Strip, and another eight smaller gambling halls, is the biggest locals chain. Boyd Gaming Corporation owns six locals casinos in Las Vegas and Henderson, the large Las Vegas suburb to the southeast, as well as three downtown casinos. These casinos have been placed strategically throughout the valley, so that residents in almost every neighborhood have convenient access to at least one.

(A few of Station's properties—including two of its priciest, Green Valley Ranch and Aliante Station—are co-owned by the Greenspun Corporation, which also owns the *Las Vegas Sun,* my employer from 2006 to 2009.)

The recession hit Station and Boyd hard. Both put significant projects on hold, and Station filed for Chapter 11 bankruptcy protection in 2009, prompting Boyd to formally express interest in buying them out. As of the date this book was sent to press, legal proceedings had not yet been resolved.

Locals casinos employ numerous tactics to lure southern Nevada residents, ranging from offering games not available on the Strip like bingo, lower-stakes blackjack tables, and "looser," higher-paying slot machines. They offer cheap dining options like fast-food outlets and perks such as comps (reward programs for frequent players) that are more generous than similar programs on the Strip, as well as check-cashing services, including tax refund check-cashing promotions.

The aim of locals casinos is not just to attract gamblers, but also to serve as sort of commercialized community centers that appeal to gamblers and non-gamblers alike, including families with young children. Every one of the dozen bowling alleys in Las Vegas and Henderson, for instance, is attached to a locals casino. Of the twenty-two multiscreen movie theater complexes in town, fourteen are inside locals casinos. Sunset Station, in an older part of Henderson east of the Strip, "contains a multiplex movie theater, an ice cream store, a supervised area for children to play, half a dozen restaurants ranging from a coffee shop to high-end dining, bars, and a nightclub, and an outdoor stage," wrote the late UNLV historian Hal Rothman in *Neon Metropolis: How Las Vegas Started the Twenty-first Century*. "It's fun and not at all threatening. There's no sense of being compelled to gamble, although a lot of people do. Instead it feels like a shopping mall. Devoid of civic space, Las Vegans use such private commercial space as public space."

Rothman was right—locals casinos have become accepted family destinations in Las Vegas, much the same way indoor shopping malls have in suburban America. Walk through a locals casino on a weekend night, especially the areas set aside for these activities, and you'll see families with school-age kids and roving groups of teens. According to Nevada state law, it's illegal for anyone under twenty-one to gamble or to "loiter, or be permitted to loiter, in or about any room or premises wherein any licensed game, race book, sports pool, or pari-mutuel wagering is operated or conducted."[4] But that line is blurred routinely in locals joints, where loudly dinging slot machines are often just feet away from theater box offices, video game arcades, pizza parlors, and child-care centers.

Station's most recent casino/hotels, Green Valley Ranch, Red Rock Resort, and Aliante Station, were built in the 2000s and are significantly more expensive than the company's other casino properties. With them, Station altered the local casino model. They cost $300 million, $1 billion, and $662 million, respectively—and were designed primarily to appeal to a certain demographic: wealthier locals, as opposed to middle-class and working-class locals. Though loaded with the same "locals" amenities, each also was built within an upscale master-planned community and is gilded with chandeliers and other posh touches, like Strip-swank pool complexes studded with palm trees.

Top Station officials have claimed they were trying to appeal to tourists as well as locals by calling Red Rock and Green Valley Ranch "destination resorts."[5] Other times, they have said bluntly that locals were their only aim. "This property is built 1,000 percent for locals," Station president Lorenzo Fertitta told the *Las Vegas Sun* during the Green Valley Ranch opening in 2001, adding, according to the article, that he was aiming primarily for the fifty-five-year-old-and-over crowd that "drives Station's fortunes."[6] When Aliante Station opened in late 2008, casino general manager Joe Hasson called his property "a resort for locals."[7]

Station, Boyd, and the other locals casinos chains and slot business operators in the region advertise relentlessly. In fact, the depressed economy prompted Station to boost its marketing efforts to record levels in 2009 and 2010. "It has everything to do with creating a value proposition to keep people coming through the door" during recessionary times, said Station executive vice president Kevin Kelley.[8]

Locals casinos tout food and gambling specials on billboards throughout the region. Their ads run routinely on TV and radio, and they contact customers through mailed promotions—especially if they have gambled at one of their properties and joined their free players' rewards clubs. Large Strip casinos employ these practices as well, targeting the local gamblers' market. Since I've moved here, rarely have more than a couple of days passed without receiving some sort of enticement by mail or e-mail to run back to a nearby casino.

As easy as it is to gamble in Las Vegas, and as impossible as it is to avoid it, there should be no surprise that gambling addiction rates there are higher as well. The industry still disputes the correlation, though it seems like common sense to most. The industry has become concerned about the increasingly accepted notion that the closer people live to gambling outlets like casinos, the more integrated those casinos are into communities, the more likely it is that people will gamble—and thus, the more likely it is that a small subset of these new gamblers will develop problems.

There is no better place to analyze this premise than Las Vegas. The most recent and comprehensive study regarding the prevalence of problem and pathological gambling in Nevada backs up the notion. The study was sponsored by the state's Department of Human Resources and published in 2002. Rachel Volberg, a top problem-gambling researcher in Massachusetts, formulated a study in which 2,200 Nevadans were given telephone surveys. The results showed higher gambling addiction rates in Nevada than in any other state that had been tested.

The survey found that just fewer than one in five adult Nevadans gambled weekly or more often. Based on the prevailing measure Volberg and others had used in several other comparable studies, problem and pathological gambling rates were significantly higher than the national mean. The study found that in 2000, 3.5 percent of the adult population could currently be classified as "probable" pathological gamblers and another 2.9 percent as the slightly less serious problem gamblers, for a total of 6.4 percent, or one out of every sixteen adult Nevadans. Based on those prevalence rates, about 88,000 adult Nevadans were hooked on gambling at the time. By 2010, that number grew to more than 115,000 people.

Four years prior, two studies were conducted that found that the combined problem/pathological gambling rates in North Dakota and Mississippi were significantly lower than Nevada's: 2.1 percent and 4.9 percent respectively. Mississippi had the second highest rates and is considered another "mature" gambling market, having had legalized casinos since 1990.

Volberg used two gambling prevalence screens for her Nevada study. The percentages referred to above were taken from the results of the South Oaks Gambling Screen (SOGS), which has long been the standard for problem gambling studies. She also used a newer screen, called the National Opinion Research Center DSM-IV Screen for Gambling Problems, commonly known as NODS. The results were similar: the current problem and pathological gambling rates in Nevada were a combined 5.1 percent with the NODS—almost twice as high as the national rate of 2.7 percent using the same screen.

The gambling industry immediately looked for ways to discount the findings of the study or represent the data more favorably for them. They noted that using the NODS results, when respondents were questioned about their gambling activities over the past year as opposed to their lifetime, the results were much lower in Nevada—a combined 2.1 percent—a percentage that was lower than the national average of 3 to 4 percent. And one Nevada Gaming Control Board member accused the SOGS screen of allowing for too many "false positives."[9]

Volberg countered that the SOGS screen was the most valid way to determine problem gambling prevalence. The same screen had been used in ten state surveys around the country (while the NODS survey had been used just once before), so it was reliable for comparison purposes.

Ultimately, Volberg's survey provides damning evidence, and it is bolstered by other types of data showing how attached Las Vegans are to gambling compared with those from other regions.

Consider Gamblers Anonymous, the nonpolitical, nonprofit twelve-step organization that provides support for problem gamblers. According to an April 2010 Las Vegas GA meeting list, there were ninety-six meetings per week in the Las Vegas Valley, including sixty in Las Vegas, thirty-five in the two suburbs Henderson and North Las Vegas, and one in Boulder City. That's fourteen meetings per day on average, held in church basements, hospital board rooms, and VA clinics around the region. On any given day, some meetings typically start as early as 8 A.M. and others end as late as 9 P.M. Fifteen of the meetings are held in Spanish.

There are more GA meetings weekly in the Las Vegas region than anywhere else in the world. In New York City's five boroughs—which contain more than four times as many people as the 1.9

million–person Las Vegas metro area—there are fifty meetings held weekly.[10] And Las Vegas's GA presence is substantially greater than in two metro areas almost identical in population, Kansas City and San Jose, California. In the Kansas City metro area, there are five weekly GA meetings. In the San Jose region, there are eight. Of course, those areas possess only a fraction of the legalized gambling Las Vegas has. But that is the point: where legalized gambling exists in greater measure, so does the need for a support program like GA.

She started gambling when she was twenty-one. In her younger days she won all the time, she said, allowing her to provide for her family and give gifts to friends. Now almost sixty, the African American woman said she's been asking others for help for a while now. Her family hates to see her because they know she'll be asking for money. It was her first GA meeting, and once she started talking, she lost control. Her voice broke and her emotions poured out, a potent blend of grief and anger. "All I've wanted to do is sleep," she said through tears. "But I told myself I can't do this anymore. I don't want to sleep. I want to go to a meeting and get help."

The Saturday afternoon GA meeting at Montevista Hospital, less than three miles due west of the Strip, is a decade old. The group allowed me to sit in on one of its June 2010 meetings on the condition that I not use any part of their names. It was a warm gathering, with a mixed group of recovering gamblers and lots of hugs between them. Twenty-six people sat in a large circle in a nondescript hospital conference room, the women slightly outnumbering the men. The group skewed toward retirement age, but there were some middle-aged and younger gamblers as well. There were African American and Asian gamblers in attendance, though most were white. Accents ran the gamut from New York and mid-Atlantic to rural Western. Two of the gamblers mentioned they were also recovering alcoholics.

The most dramatic moment involved that first-time attendee.

Her story held the rapt attention of the other recovering gamblers, at least one of whom had been in the program for more than two decades. Several offered their support, saying they had once been in her shoes. As others got their turn to speak, one older gentleman said that living in Las Vegas, "surrounded by slot machines," made it tougher to quit gambling and to stay away from it. A different man said soon after: "We're blessed here. It's easy to gamble, but it's easy to find recovery, too."

Another recovering gambler, a woman in her mid-seventies, was a poker dealer for casinos on the Strip and downtown Las Vegas for about thirty years. She gambled during her off hours, often to excess. She told a brutal story about how her addiction drove her to attempt suicide. She had maxed out eight credit cards, sold most everything she owned, and in 2007, purchased a gun. She aimed for her heart but missed by an inch. She has been in recovery from her gambling addiction for three years.

"I bought this chair with almost my life," she said.

In the most significant study to date on the consequences of gambling addiction in southern Nevada, researchers at UNLV in 2003 put a price tag on the social costs that resulted from the abundance of addicted gamblers. Ninety-nine surveys completed by Las Vegas area GA members gauged how much the gamblers had lost. The researchers broke down the cost of their gambling, including the outstanding debts and bankruptcies filed; crimes committed including theft and embezzlement; criminal justice system costs resulting from those crimes; lowered work productivity and increased social welfare costs, including food stamps, welfare, and unemployment insurance; and the cost of treating their addiction. In Clark County, the social costs from problem and pathological gamblers ranged between $301 million and $469 million.[11]

The researchers used certain methodologies to ensure that the numbers would not be inflated. "[W]e suggest that our estimates are conservative and below what the real social costs are," the study's authors wrote. The actual total social cost could fairly be estimated to be as high as $900 million per year, said UNLV professor and report coauthor William N. Thompson.[12] The results apply to only locally based gamblers and not tourists.

The survey confirmed the unique nature of the population of Las Vegas problem gamblers. More than four out of five questioned said they had gambled at a locals casino; just over one in two said they had gone to the Strip to gamble. About 40 percent said they gambled in bars, taverns, convenience stores, and supermarkets. One in three respondents worked in the casino industry, a percentage that correlates with what the study's authors note is the fact that one-third of southern Nevada's employment base consists of jobs in the casino/hotel industry. "It also may suggest a major occupational hazard for employees who are constantly exposed to gambling activity," the authors wrote.

More recently, Thompson and a different UNLV colleague wrote what can be described as an outraged appeal for civic-mindedness for one of Las Vegas's daily newspapers, in which they attacked the region's gambling-crazed citizenry for willingly getting sucked up into "a crisis of greed, selfishness and stupidity."[13] The well-known, to-the-grave resistance of Nevadans to tax themselves "will decimate the university system and public education and shred other public protections" once federal stimulus funds dry up in 2011, wrote Thompson and article coauthor William M. Epstein, a social work professor. They decried the fact that while Nevadans' reluctance to pony up has led to some of the weakest education, child welfare, and health-related public services in the country, at the same time, the average Clark County adult incurs gambling losses of $1,511 per year (compared with American adult gambling losses averaging $391 per year). This kind of local culture suits the gambling industry just fine, they conclude: "The hustler's view of life explains in large part the civic depravity of the state. The problem is not gambling per se but rather the Nevadans who gamble, the corporations that prey on gambling and the corrosive ethos they create."

Bo Bernhard, a top problem gambling researcher at UNLV, is a fifth-generation Las Vegan. "I grew up in the shadows of this town," he said, referring to his childhood home about five miles northeast of the old heart of the Strip. While studying at Harvard in the early 1990s, he was asked by a psychology professor to examine problem gamblers in Las Vegas. That assignment metamorphosed into his undergraduate thesis, and eventually, after receiving his doctorate at UNLV, his life's work. He's become a nationally recognized expert on problem gambling and the author of numerous studies and papers on the topic.

Bernhard is the son of Peter Bernhard, a white-shoe business litigation attorney who in 2001 was appointed to become chairman of the Nevada Gaming Commission, the state's main gambling industry regulatory and policy making body. His second full term is set to expire in 2011. Bo Bernhard said that his father's positions on gambling-related issues have not influenced the types of research that he has taken on. (As it so happens, Bo Bernhard isn't the only prominent advocate for problem gamblers in Las Vegas with strong connections to the gambling industry.) As he told the *Las Vegas Review-Journal* in 2008: "I'm torn. I believe in my Nevada soul that a gaming industry that's regulated properly, licensed, subjected to the rigors, is a good thing. But I'm also sensitive to the problem gambler and the underage gambler."[14]

It is that sensitivity, coupled with his training, that led Bo to conduct a significant study into the long-term health of problem gamblers in Nevada, Arizona, and Nebraska who have received treatment. The study, called the Nevada Problem Gambling Project, examined the results of 449 interviews with problem gambling treatment recipients, two-thirds of whom were from Nevada. They found that treatment in one of the state's six outpatient problem gambling treatment centers, often coupled with GA attendance, had an excellent success rate. Ninety-five percent of those treated reported that they had cut down their gambling from the period in which they gambled most heavily—"a strikingly, overwhelmingly positive finding," Bernhard concluded in a report.[15]

"One of the good parts of this tale is that there's a great treatment scene here," Bo told me. "We're in a much better place in Las Vegas from a treatment perspective in contrast to a generation ago." He is reluctant to sign on to the notion that Las Vegas has been irreparably damaged as a community because of the pervasive gambling, or that communities that expand their legalized gambling options necessarily are hurt over the long haul. "I'm skeptical of the notion that availability equals doom," he said.

However, there is countless data suggesting that Las Vegas is nothing short of the dysfunction capital of America—and that that dysfunction comes in part from the omnipresence of gambling. The region leads the nation in crime, home foreclosure, and suicide rates. It is fair to conclude that this is somewhat closely related to the high rates of problem gambling. What follows is just a portion of the most compelling research.

Nevada was rated the most dangerous state in the nation seven recent years in a row, from 2004 to 2010. The rankings from CQ Press are determined using the rates of six different crime categories —murder, rape, aggravated assault, robbery, burglary, and auto theft—and then comparing those rates to the national average. In 2010, Nevada's murder rate was more than six times as high as the survey's safest state, New Hampshire, and it topped the country-wide list for robberies, with roughly 250 reported cases per 100,000 residents.[16]

There is a proven link between gambling addiction and robbery. A 2004 U.S. Justice Department report studied this link in both Las Vegas and Des Moines, Iowa. Researchers interviewed more than two thousand arrestees in jail about their gambling habits. They found that a total of 14 percent of the arrestees in Vegas were either problem or pathological gamblers, more than twice as high as the percentage of addicted gamblers in the general population. More than 30 percent of the pathological gamblers arrested in both cities said they had committed a robbery within the past year—and nearly a third of them said they had committed the robbery to fund their gambling or to pay gambling debts.[17]

Along with a high crime rate, Nevada had the highest percentage of home foreclosures in the nation from 2007 through early 2010. The Las Vegas metro area alone also held the top spot in the country in the first quarter of 2010. More than twenty-eight thousand housing units in Las Vegas received a foreclosure filing during the quarter. That meant one in twenty-eight housing units received such a filing—almost five times the national average.[18] In a study on home foreclosures, researchers with the Federal Deposit Insurance Corporation noted the rise in the number of Americans who gambled at casinos, which, "when practiced in excess, can easily lead to insolvency."[19]

Gambling industry officials have scoffed at the idea that problem gambling has led to foreclosures. "People are not gambling away their mortgages," said Harrah's Entertainment Senior Vice President Jan Jones, formerly the mayor of Las Vegas, in 2008.[20] Michele Johnson, CEO of the Las Vegas–based Consumer Credit Counseling Service, the only nonprofit credit counseling service in the state, disagrees. She told me in an interview that about 6 percent of the consumers that come to her group "are honest about the fact that gambling is the main cause or a contributing factor" of their situation. And there are many others who are not forthcoming about gambling being the cause of their debt. Johnson does believe that some southern Nevadans are, in fact, gambling away their mortgages. "Absolutely, we see this happening. Anecdotally, it's not a huge percentage of the cases we see. But does it come into play? No question, it does," she said. For that matter, Johnson's assertion could quite easily be backed up by attending just one or two of the scores of weekly GA meetings in the region.

Bankruptcy is another consequence of problem gambling, and Nevada led the nation in bankruptcy filings in the fiscal year ending September 30, 2009, with more than twenty-seven thousand filed. Nevadans filed at a rate of 10.49 filings per one thousand people—more than twice the national rate.[21] In fiscal 2008, Nevada ranked second highest in the country. Also in late 2009, the credit reporting company TransUnion reported that Nevada led the way in the company's third-quarter 2009 credit card delinquency statistics. That meant more Nevadans per capita were ninety days or more delinquent on at least one of their credit cards than anywhere else in the country.[22]

Several studies over the last fifteen years have shown unequivocally that bankruptcy rates are higher in counties where there are casinos and other gambling outlets than in counties farther away from gambling. Frank Fahrenkopf Jr. of the American Gaming Association acknowledged in a 2001 *Las Vegas Sun* story that communities with casinos "often" have higher bankruptcy rates. However, he attempted to explain this away by pointing out that such communities attract people looking for a "fresh start." When those fresh starts fail, trouble occurs. "That doesn't mean they filed for bankruptcy because there are casinos in the community," he said.[23]

Divorce is also perpetuated by the presence of legal gambling. After Cheyenne, Wyoming, Las Vegas is the city where married residents are most likely "doomed for divorce," according to the June 2010 edition of *Men's Health* magazine. They tallied their results based on the state's lenient divorce laws, the high divorce rate, and the low number of family and marriage counselors in the region.[24]

Of course, Nevada historically has had famously lenient divorce laws. But there is also a strong nexus between divorces and problem gambling. The lifetime divorce rate for problem and pathological gamblers is more than twice that of non-gamblers. The impact of addictive gambling also hurts gamblers' families in several other ways, including spousal and child abuse. A 2007 study conducted by psychiatrists in Las Vegas and at the University of Iowa concluded that not only are high rates of separation and divorce well-documented, but "data from a variety of sources converge to paint a picture of the pathological gambler's family as disturbed and chaotic. . . . [C]lose relatives frequently suffer from mental health or addictive disorders."[25]

One of the most grave consequences of problem gambling is suicide. For years, Nevada has had the highest suicide rate in the country, roughly twice the national average. A 2008 study led by a former UNLV researcher confirmed that residents of Clark County, home to Las Vegas, were more than 50 percent more likely to commit suicide than other Americans. What's more, when Clark County residents (especially men) left Las Vegas, their likelihood of committing suicide dropped by 13 to 40 percent.[26] The authors did not draw conclusions as to precisely why this was the case. They wrestled with conflicting notions, including the thought that the rate might be especially high in Las Vegas because of the inordinately high amounts of gambling, as well as the twenty-four-hour access to addictive substances like alcohol and drugs, and a lack of mental health resources. They also noted—as have others searching for reasons why Las Vegas seems plagued with communal problems—that it could be the case that people who are more impulsive or generally predisposed to risk, traits causing an increased threat of suicide, seek out Sin City.

Both explanations may be at least partially true. A 2007 study by the *Las Vegas Sun*, based on data from the Centers for Disease Control and Prevention, showed that the rate of suicides among senior citizens in Nevada is astonishing; it is not only the highest rate in the country, but nearly three times the national average. From 1999 to 2004, the rate of suicides among those seventy-five and older was forty-eight per one hundred thousand. According to the report, 279 seniors in that age group committed suicide statewide; of those, 169 took their lives in Clark County. In total, almost two of every three of the 2,661 suicides in the state during the six-year period took place in Clark County.[27]

Problem gambling among Las Vegas–area seniors is a factor in their high suicide rates, experts have concluded. And there is no doubt that many seniors move to Las Vegas specifically to gamble: a 2007 study determined that one in four seniors aged fifty-five to ninety moved to Clark County from out of state in whole or in part because of increased gambling opportunities.[28]

Gambling has had other harmful impacts on the Las Vegas community. It's one of several reasons why the local homelessness problem is intractable. "I run across a lot of problem gamblers in the program, and it's been an issue of increasing concern," said Alretta Harris, residential work program supervisor with Catholic Charities of Southern Nevada. Harris's program provides safe housing and meals for three hundred able-bodied homeless men, as well as counseling and job training. For years, that counseling included drug and alcohol addiction sessions three days a week, to raise awareness and target those who need help. One week before I called her, Harris said she added problem gambling training sessions to the treatment. She's also begun referring five to eight men in her program per week to Gamblers Anonymous.

Harris noted that some of the homeless gamblers at her shelter give casinos their temporary Catholic Charities address when they sign up for frequent player programs. That has led to a stream of free- or reduced-bet promotions flooding into the facility from local gambling chains and Strip giants, which makes it even more difficult for the men to stay away. "We get a tremendous amount of mail from the casinos, and that's added to the problem," she said.

There have been few, if any, formal studies examining the link between legalized gambling and the payday loan and pawnbroker industries. But critics of all three businesses have long claimed the latter two feed directly off of addicted gamblers, who turn to pawnshops and payday loan stores for easy ways to raise funds to pay gambling debts and to replenish their gambling bankrolls. Several states in recent years have battled the payday loan industry, ultimately banning such stores, because of concerns about exorbitant interest rates and the notion that they target poor customers with little ability to pay off their loans without costly extensions.

In a 2009 report prepared for the payday loan industry trade group called the Community Financial Services Association of America, Nevada was listed as having "high positive growth" in the number of payday stores in 2007. According to the report, the industry in Nevada contributed about $158 million to the gross state product (GSP) and ranked fourteenth highest in the country in terms of how much the industry contributed as a percentage of the GSP.[29] A spokesman for the National Pawnbrokers Association, Emmett Murphy, said figures about the industry's size in Nevada compared with other states were not available. But he rejected the notion that there is a strong correlation between problem gamblers and the pawnshop industry. "We're really there to provide safety net loans to those who need them," he said.

In the July 2009 Embarq Yellow Pages, there were listings for sixty-two pawnshops in the Las Vegas Valley—and for another 191 payday or similar "signature" loan stores. From a ground-level view, they loom even larger. It is difficult to drive through any commercial strip in Las Vegas without passing at least one or two payday loan and pawnshops; they seem as ubiquitous as fast-food outlets.

The situation is similar in northern Nevada. "[E]vidence of problem gambling abounds with a very visible array of pawn shops and payday loan centers, which attach themselves to casinos like parasites," wrote Guy Farmer, a columnist for the *Nevada Appeal* newspaper in Carson City, in 2007. "We don't need more casinos and payday loan offices in our historic capital city; instead, we need solid retail establishments, and that's what city officials should be seeking."[30] Farmer knows the gambling industry from the inside. Several decades ago, he was the first public information officer for the Nevada Gaming Commission.

For twenty-three consecutive years until 2007, Nevada had been among the top four states in population growth, with most of that growth occurring in the Las Vegas Valley. Since that year, Las Vegas has grown at a slower rate. Clark County had a population of just over 1.9 million in July of 2009, a relatively paltry 1.3 percent hike from the year before. Still, since the 2000 census, the region grew by more than a half-million people.

The population shift seen in Las Vegas, where people were simultaneously leaving the area at about half the rate of those moving in, makes for a highly transient community. Many new residents feel disconnected and unwilling to consider the region home. Because few people feel a strong sense of community, there have been consistently low levels of volunteering in Las Vegas. As tallied by the Corporation for National and Community Service, the region scored the third-to-lowest volunteering rate in the country in 2009 out of fifty-one regions studied.[31]

What's more, a large number of those who have flooded the region relocated for low-skill but relatively high-paying jobs in the casino/hotel business. This has prevented the local economy from diversifying as much as analysts say it needs to and has helped keep college education levels for adults low compared with the rest of the country. A 2009 survey by the website the *Daily Beast,* which looked at "America's smartest cities," showed just how low.[32] The site ranked the top fifty-five metropolitan areas on the basis of several factors, including how many residents had bachelors and graduate degrees; how well nonfiction books sold in the region; the ratio of colleges and universities in the area; and the percentage of eligible voters who cast ballots in the 2008 presidential election. Las Vegas finished second to last. Only Fresno, California, was considered less smart. The national indignity only grew the following year. In the *Daily Beast*'s 2010 survey, which used slightly modified criteria, Vegas ranked dead dumbest.

Yet the constant stream of new arrivals from other parts of the country also has meant that the state once considered "the Mississippi of the West" for its retrograde attitudes toward civil rights is becoming more ethnically diverse and less conservative. In 2008, the state voted to send Barack Obama to the White House—only the third time in the last ten presidential elections that Nevada's voters chose the Democratic candidate. As of June 2010, Democrats held a 110,000 voter-registration advantage in the state.

Despite the changing attitudes of its populace, Nevada officials were among the last in the country to accept any responsibility toward the state's problem gamblers. In the decade before 2005, when the legislature finally passed a bill to provide funding to assist addicted gamblers, advocates regularly were snubbed when trying to persuade lawmakers that gambling addiction was a public health issue. Nor were legislators convinced that it was cheaper in the long run to treat problem gamblers and to try to prevent their addiction in the first place, than it is to have the state pick up the tab for all of the increased social costs stemming from it. Instead, supporters were faced with long-held attitudes that problem gamblers were solely to blame for their own predicaments. In the early years of the fight, said Bo Bernhard, "We were confronted in Carson City with, 'Why should we give money to help degenerate gamblers?'"

Other states have funded efforts to aid problem gamblers since the early 1970s. By the time Nevada agreed to provide funding in 2005, over thirty other states already had decided to devote funds to similar programs—in most cases hundreds of thousands or millions of dollars annually—despite the fact that they had just a fraction of the legalized gambling as Nevada. As of June 2010, thirty-eight states allocated public funds toward programs to aid problem gamblers.[33]

The Nevada bill provided $2.5 million over two years, including $1.5 million in grants set aside for seven treatment providers. The funds came from a small portion of state revenues from slot machine licensing fees.

For several years before the bill passed, proponents were backed by tourism officials and Nevada's powerful gambling industry, the tax on which, as of 2007, provided 28 percent of all revenues for the state's general fund. By then, the industry—looking to be seen as both responsible and ahead of the curve—had taken a few modest steps to help problem gamblers. Though Nevada Gaming Commission regulations stipulate that gambling licensees train employees who come in contact with customers about the issue, major casino operators went beyond that in small ways. MGM Mirage mandated that their properties begin displaying messages about gambling addiction in employee areas like dining halls, for example. Harrah's Entertainment created an "exclusion list" that allowed gamblers to request that they stop receiving all casino comps and the ability to gamble on credit. Both of these gambling giants, as well as Station Casinos and many other industry operators, also have donated to the Problem Gambling Center in Las Vegas and the Nevada Council on Problem Gambling.

The recession hit tourism-dependant Las Vegas as hard as any region in the country. Las Vegas used to be known as "last in and first out" of economic downturns. But this time, analysts believe the region will be one of the last to climb out of the morass because of its devastated local housing market. Both the biggest Strip casinos and locals chains were rocked by the downturn, which caused profits to plummet and gambling stocks to shrink to next to nothing before rebounding in 2010. Several high-profile casino and condominium projects on the Strip were put on hold, mid-construction. Since the beginning of the recession through mid-2009, about five thousand workers with the Culinary Union, which represents restaurant and hotel workers in most Strip resorts, either lost their jobs or had their hours reduced.[34]

The economic downturn also took a significant toll on the state's funding efforts to aid problem gamblers—and at the same time, spurred efforts to expand gambling's reach even further throughout Nevada.

In reaction to the state's severe budget woes, Governor Jim Gibbons proposed scrapping all of the state's funding for problem gambling treatment, and he almost succeeded in early 2010. After a bout of feverish lobbying by problem gambler advocates, lawmakers agreed to cut what would amount to about $350,000, instead of the whole $850,000 program. The advocates were greatly relieved. As one of them told me, it will be much easier to convince legislators to add money to an existing program than to kick-start a new one.

As the recession caused legislators to cut aid for problem gambling, gambling proponents simultaneously advanced several efforts to make the activity more available to Nevadans. At a gaming law conference in 2008, the general counsel for Aristocrat Technologies, a slot machine manufacturer, asked state gaming regulators to suggest to state lawmakers that the minimum gambling age be lowered from twenty-one to eighteen. State Gaming Control Board chair Dennis Neilander agreed to forward the suggestion, which was ultimately shot down by state leaders.

In another expansion effort, legislators in 2009 pushed for a state lottery. It was the twenty-seventh time since 1975 that proponents unsuccessfully promoted a lottery bill. Nevada is one of only seven states without a lottery—in large part because of the consistent opposition of the locals casino industry, would-be competitors for the same customer base. In 2007, Boyd Gaming and Station Casinos jointly unveiled a study that found that a state lottery would create 316 new jobs in Nevada, but it also would eliminate 595 jobs in the gaming and hospitality industry. At a 2009 legislative hearing, Russell Rowe, a lobbyist for Boyd, said lotteries, with their astronomical odds against winning, are sometimes described as "a tax on stupidity."[35]

Though industry hired guns like Rowe may be quick to ridicule some types of gamblers, it's doubtful they would ever include Las Vegas mayor Oscar Goodman. The savvy and popular mayor of more than a decade is the biggest local booster of all that is Vegas. It's been theorized that Goodman, who is also chairman of the board of the Las Vegas Convention and Visitors Authority, happily talks about his gin drinking and showgirl accessorizing in large part to promote regional tourism. Regardless, he's better known for those things than he is for his gambling.

But on more than one occasion he has alluded to the notion that he is a serious gambler. He was forthright about his wagering habits in an essay he wrote for *Esquire* magazine in 2004 in which he said he gambles "with both fists" and noted that he even used to bet on which way a City Hall basement–dwelling cockroach would run. "I'll play a couple hands. I'll put a little money in the slot machine. I don't know how to play craps even to this day," he wrote. "But what I am is a degenerate sports bettor. During the daytime, I have all the action I can handle. But at night, when I'm sleeping, I need something going on. I need to wake up to something and see how I did."[36]

While covering Goodman's administration for the *Las Vegas Sun* from 2008 to 2009, I noticed that during City Council meetings and press conferences the mayor often joked about his football and basketball bets. In September 2008, he proposed to a Las Vegas sports radio station that the National Football League existed primarily as a platform for betting. "The NFL, you know, wouldn't be the NFL but for the fact that gambling took place," he said.[37] "And I'll tell you this: I couldn't watch a game without having a bet on it."

When I pressed him for a few particulars about his betting habits one time, he played it coy. After a press event ended, I approached Goodman and asked him where he places his bets, and how often and how much he typically wagers on games. I was mostly just curious, but I also knew that if he agreed to share some details, it would have made for a good story. The former high-priced criminal defense lawyer deflected the question. I then suggested that my paper's readers, especially the gamblers among them, might be interested to learn more about the wagering he's long hinted at. "I'm sure they would, Mr. Skolnik," he said, smiling, as he left the press area with his security detail and a couple of aides in tow.

Take just one step outside the front door of the building that houses the Nevada Council on Problem Gambling, and the view is breathtaking. Turn to the east and you are immediately hit with a close-in, skyline view of many of the biggest Las Vegas Strip mega-casinos that draw millions to the region every year. Bellagio. Caesars Palace. The Mirage.

Carol O'Hare has run the council since 1996, and she is nothing short of passionate about her job. An addicted gambler with almost twenty years in recovery, aiding other problem gamblers has become her life's work.

We talked for several hours at her office. O'Hare wore round glasses and shoulder-length light brown hair with small streaks of gray, and her expression sometimes became stern when we disagreed. She is razor sharp, and spoke in long, energetic bursts as she worked to convince me of the merits of her arguments. Her feet circled beneath her as she talked.

The first part of her tale is gripping, but sadly it isn't unique. Like many others, O'Hare fell into a gambling addiction after moving to Las Vegas. A self-described military brat, she was raised by "normal, nonaddicted" parents who were active with their Southern Baptist faith. She moved to the region with her family in 1986, when she was thirty, to be closer to her parents and a brother who lived here. Soon after the move, she and her husband began heading out to a nearby locals casino "sporadically," just the two of them, as a way to get away from their kids for a while. They started going more often to eat dinner, see a movie, or hear music. She said they very quickly found that it functioned as "a neighborhood place."

Unfortunately, their marriage was strained and their finances were worsening, and O'Hare decided to find a job. This gave her more flexibility to go back to the casino when she wanted—and the sense that it was okay to be out on her own and to play her favorite video poker games when she wanted. "I had to answer to no one, and I'd never had that feeling before, that complete and total sense that I've separated myself from every stressful thing that makes my life difficult," she said. "I had suspended life."

O'Hare and her husband finalized their divorce in 1989, and she broke down. For the next eighteen months, her gambling took on an ever more important role in her life, and she spiraled downward. While she was still working, she could gamble eight to twelve hours at a time, go home and grab one hour of sleep, then head back to work. "My job was to work for eight hours a day, then come home and do the evening hours of motherhood, you know, feed them, bathe them, make sure the homework was done. And then, when they're all in bed, now then my time starts," she said.

When she hit bottom, she was gambling whenever she could put her hands on money, sometimes fifteen to twenty hours straight at a stretch. She was unemployed, had eviction notices on her door, and was borrowing money from everyone who was willing to take her calls. Her kids were wearing clothes she took from her church's donation bin. She believed she still pretty much looked like a normal person, but later she realized that people saw her as someone breaking down. She started to convince herself that suicide was a better way to care for her children. Family members would step in to raise them, she rationalized.

Thankfully, before that happened, O'Hare quit gambling, on January 31, 1991. She hasn't placed a bet since.

This is where her story takes a uniquely Las Vegas twist.

While working on her recovery through Gamblers Anonymous, O'Hare's boyfriend, who later became her second husband, taught her how the casino business works, giving her an inside look at how casino gambling floors function. (He is currently a thirty-year veteran casino floorman at a major Strip resort, but she wouldn't say which one.) At the same time, she took a job at an insurance company, where she felt forced to hide what was the most valuable part of her life—her recovery from gambling. She knew it was a socially stigmatized condition from the talk around her office, including scathing remarks she overheard about the district manager's wife being a "degenerate gambler."

"I hid my addiction," O'Hare said. "I lived two lives with my addiction. I was like, you know, Carol Black, Carol White. I didn't want to live that way in my recovery. I didn't want to go to work and feel like I was doing the shifty-eyed thing to make sure a piece of GA literature didn't fall out of my purse. And so that's when my external views started to develop.

"Somebody should be talking about this!" she said, shaking her head. "Somebody should be talking about this."

O'Hare met with Howie C. after a GA meeting in 1993 and agreed to help out with the then-fledgling state problem gambling council. Later that year, a Harrah's executive named Dennis Conrad called the council. Harrah's was hosting one of its five-day Harrah's Institutes in Las Vegas for some of the company's non-casino hotel managers to learn the gambling side of the business. Conrad wanted a woman gambler—a video poker player, specifically—to address the institute because Harrah's was attracting more women gamblers to their new riverboat casinos.

O'Hare agreed to speak to the group. Her presentation, which spared no details about her addiction, shocked them. "I was hooked on the idea that there's some value to this," she said. She agreed to continue to speak to the groups on a volunteer basis, in return for a Harrah's contribution to the council. About six months later, in 1994, Conrad said Harrah's wanted her to work for them full-time. At the time, the company was being grilled about problem gambling by several state legislatures weighing whether to legalize gambling.

She signed a two-year contract to go to different state capitals and tell her story. But before she agreed, she had to sell the idea to the National Council on Problem Gambling. She was a recovering gambler active with GA, involved with the state-affiliate Nevada problem gambling council—and also wanted to work on contract for Harrah's, meaning, The Industry. Though some in the national council were openly hostile to the idea, O'Hare said the majority understood her hopes to change the industry by working from the inside. They allowed her to stay affiliated with the Nevada council while working for Harrah's.

As a consultant, she trained Harrah's officials about problem gambling, worked on policy issues, and did media and legislative work. She went to the sites of state legislative battles, worked the local media, and testified before legislative committees. But she said she never advocated for legalizing Harrah's proposed casinos. "Harrah's didn't hire me to tell other people their view of problem gambling. My contract very specifically said that I was going to be their consultant. I would provide education about problem gambling, I would provide input and expertise to assist them in developing and improving their programs to address problem gambling, and I would speak publicly about the reality of problem gambling. No way was I going to be the Harrah's mouthpiece."

Another Harrah's mission for O'Hare was to turn the Nevada

Council on Problem Gambling into a viable organization that the company could support, she said. That included getting donation pledges from other gambling companies, since state funding was then nonexistent. Several came on board. When the time came to choose the group's new executive director, O'Hare was the logical choice.

Every problem gambling council around the country, including the national council, is responsible for speaking out on behalf of the needs of problem gamblers, including making sure adequate services to prevent and treat problem gamblers are funded and maintained. This includes discussing the possible impacts of expanded gambling with politicians or the media. But the state and national councils must remain neutral on legalized gambling expansion proposals. They will not take a stand on political and legislative efforts to add slot machines to a local racetrack, for example, or whether to insti-tute a new state lottery. This stems from the council's background in the gambling recovery community, and its beliefs that taking in-dividual responsibility and not blaming others are vital to being able to make a sustained recovery. Yet O'Hare is zealous about her neu-trality. It is a "mathematical fact," she said, that if you increase the opportunity to gamble there will be more problem gamblers. But focusing on that notion alone diminishes her belief that problem gamblers have a mental health disorder, "that is more a product of them than it is of their environment." So targeting the availabil-ity of gambling as the only cause of problem gamblers is faulty, she said.

"You know, I'm sitting in GA meetings, and they're telling me, 'You can't blame your history, you can't blame your family, you can't blame your ex-husband.' And I just added one more thing to the list. I went, 'Well, I don't think I can blame the casinos, then, can I? That's not logical,'" said O'Hare.

"I was in a deteriorating state of some kind long before gambling came into the picture," she said. "All addicts are."

•   •   •

Three months after I interviewed O'Hare, she told gambling industry marketers at a casino marketing conference that it was okay to
advertise to customers who exhibited addictive gambling behavior—so long as the marketing pitches focused on the property's
non-gambling amenities and didn't provide them betting coupons or
other incentives to gamble.[38] She noted that three out of four casino
customers eat at casino restaurants and often also see shows or visit
bars or clubs on the property. "I am a consumer with discretionary
income, an active member of the community, a person who enjoys
having fun with friends and family and a non-gambler by choice,"
she said. "But I am potentially your customer, too."

After meeting some of the gamblers who signed up for treatment
at the Problem Gambling Center in Las Vegas—usually gamblers
near their lowest state, new to their recovery, reeling from their addiction, and desperate to stay away from casinos—it seems clear that
they would not want to receive any casino flyers in the mail, whether
the coupons were for a free hamburger or $10 in free slot machine
play. The center is the busiest gambling treatment center in Nevada.
The center's intensive outpatient program—which costs a total of
$145, a fee that's usually waived because of financial hardship—is
six-weeks long and has had a short waiting list for years. Four days
per week there are group therapy sessions led by the center's clinical
director Robert Hunter, a psychologist, followed by lectures from
Hunter on different topics one day a week. In addition, outpatient
program participants must attend at least two GA meetings per week,
fill out workbooks and questionnaires in order to aid their recovery,
and can request to have a one-on-one session with a counselor. Several of the staffers are recovering problem gamblers who have at least
two years without a bet. According to the center's executive director,
counselors there treated 250 gamblers in the outpatient program in

2009, and another six 660 seniors, in part stemming from outreach programs to senior homes.

The outpatient program has a fairly high dropout rate. About 20 percent of the participants miss the second meeting after showing up for the first, and of those who come back a second time, one-third of them leave before the program is halfway finished.

Hunter allowed me access to one of the program's group meetings in April 2010, which had similarities to a GA meeting, including the condition that I not use any names or identifying characteristics of the gamblers. There were nineteen recovering gamblers in attendance. Hunter went around the room to gauge their progress. The length of time in recovery of many of the participants was shorter than in GA meetings. Many of these gamblers had been away from the tables and slot machines for days, not yet months or years. Also, the average participant seemed younger than most of those at the GA meeting at Montevista Hospital.

One soft-spoken young man in a T-shirt and shorts talked about how he made his last bet about one month before. Now, he said, getting treatment was of paramount importance. Despite the fact that his one-year-old son was sick and in the hospital, he said even his wife knew that for these six weeks, it was more important that he receive treatment than anything else.

Another man, a generation older, said he had placed his last bet just five days before and that this was his first group meeting. Clean-cut and conservatively dressed, he seemed about as uncomfortable sharing his feelings with strangers as possible. He said he was there because he had been dipping into his son's college fund to support his gambling, and enough was enough. "I'm exhausted, embarrassed, ashamed. I don't know how to stop," he said.

Afterward, Hunter, a nationally respected expert on the topic, spoke about how gambling addicts have distorted senses of control and responsibility. The good news is that with recovery, "appropriate thinking" can take hold. With recovery, he said, you don't turn into who you were right before you started gambling. You turn into the person you're supposed to be.

If Hunter's notion is right, then his former longtime colleague Howie C. reverted to his prerecovery frame of mind when he went back out gambling in March 2009.

As Howie talks, it's hard not to conclude that this is the case. He had a difficult time explaining exactly why he went back to gambling, especially now, after thirty-seven-plus years of abstinence, when he had "everything in my life the way somebody would want it." He said that when he thought about gambling again in the days leading up to the March Madness college basketball playoffs, he weighed everything he had to lose, including how his years of recovery would sink with that first bet.

That's why it had to be enormous, Howie said. He wanted to make it a sufficiently big bet so that a win would make it all worth it. But he lost. After that, he went straight to the bank to finance a bet on another game—a bet big enough to cover his first. He lost that one, too, and then several more sports bets in a row. He declined to say exactly how much he had wagered.

"I was crazy, immediately," Howie said. "I lost more money in those first two bets than I've ever lost in my whole life in any one day or week or month."

He now plays low-stakes poker regularly and makes occasional sports wagers. He doesn't discount the possibility that he'll head back into GA someday. He realizes that until that happens the majority of his friends from the program likely will disappear. The day before our interview, Howie said he got a call from his GA sponsor in Colorado, who told Howie that he needed to cut off communication with him because his own recovery was being put in jeopardy by maintaining contact.

For now, Howie is about where he was when he moved to Las Vegas. If he just keeps working at it, he believes he can gamble and win. The corners of his eyes turned downward as he explained this. Sorrow crept into his gaze, belying his optimistic words.

He noted how he bet too much recently on a Los Angeles Lakers playoff game because he was chasing gambling losses from earlier that day. "I went home saying I've got to be different. I'm trying to learn from this constantly, on a daily basis," said Howie. "I've got to say no, tomorrow's another day. There's plenty of action here all the time. Tomorrow's another day. Go home. Tomorrow's another day. A compulsive gambler can't do that."

Before he began his recovery, Howie said he always told people that gambling can be beat. It takes three components—knowledge of the game, money management skills, and control.

"I've got knowledge of the game and I've got the money management down," he said. "But I have to get control."

CHAPTER 3

The Asian Connection

Angela L. first gambled when she was twelve. During her family's Chinese New Year's celebrations in Taipei, children traditionally received red envelopes filled with cash. "The red envelope is like a Christmas gift," she said. Afterward, the kids were encouraged to gamble with their newfound riches, playing card games and mahjongg, a game of matching tiles.

As she grew older, her parents warned her to avoid gambling. By the time she moved to Los Angeles in 1985, though Angela had friends and family members who gambled regularly, she had heeded her parents' advice. It was tradition, and an important part of her culture, but she'd been able to maintain her distance from it.

That changed when Angela—who spoke on condition that her last name not be revealed—moved while in her early thirties. As she became hooked, as gambling became the dominant force in her life for a dozen years, she has no doubt that her background hastened and intensified her addiction. Being Taiwanese and ethnically Chinese, she said, laid the groundwork for her descent.

I spoke with Angela, a southern California–based tour guide, while she was taking a break from one of her twice-monthly, two-day trips to Las Vegas. We met at Caesars Palace, where her tour group had assembled, before I drove her back to her hotel, the more modest Riviera. She guided me to the Riviera by a surprisingly speedy backstreet route I would've guessed only cabbies knew. We chatted over iced tea and lemonade at Kady's, the casino's twenty-four-hour coffee shop.

Now in her mid-fifties, Angela spoke in a heavily accented English. She told her story in a high-pitched voice and had an energy found in many long-time recovering gamblers that seemed both confident and slightly anxious.

After moving to the United States and beginning her work as a tour guide in 1989, Angela had lots of downtime during her regular Las Vegas trips and began playing the slot machines, small amounts at first, to pass the time. She'd spend $20 to $50, and if she lost it she'd walk away. In the early 1990s, as her marriage became increasingly strained, her gambling intensified. One-dollar slot machines were replaced by $5 machines. She grew fond of blackjack and pai gow, a Chinese game of numbered tiles she was already familiar with. The games felt easy to fall into, aided by the camaraderie she found with the other Asian players and dealers.

She had an increasingly tough time stopping when she was losing. Soon, her working trips to Vegas became gambling binges. On some trips, she gambled for more than forty-eight hours straight. "Many times, I didn't sleep one minute," Angela said.

She also regularly gambled while at home with a group of fellow Taiwanese expatriates. They played a card game they called Russian poker. Players won or lost as much as $1,000 per session. (Among non-Chinese, the game is typically called "Chinese poker.")

By the end, when Angela first contacted Gamblers Anonymous after a brutal Las Vegas trip in April of 2000 left her devastated and penniless, she had amassed $50,000 in credit lines at three prominent Strip hotels—and had lost a total of $700,000. She was forced to file for bankruptcy after taking out three mortgages on her home to raise gambling funds and pay debts. She borrowed money from any friend or family member who would loan to her. Her marriage melted down, and her relationship with her daughter became badly strained. She thought about suicide but never attempted it. After relapsing twice, Angela quit gambling for good on October 24, 2001.

Initially, having to come back to Las Vegas for her job was brutally tough. She remembers one time while staying at the Imperial Palace, an older, Asian-themed casino in the middle of the Strip. She had finished with her tour group for the night and desperately wanted to get back to her room and away from the temptations of the casino floor. But as she walked through the casino, she couldn't find the elevator. Tears streamed down her face as she wandered past banks of blinking slot machines and busy blackjack tables, lost. "It really hurt," she said. "It was the consequences of the behavior—I know it made me want to kill myself, so I couldn't do it again."

Angela credits Gamblers Anonymous with saving her. Recognizing how easy it was for those with her background to develop gambling habits, she decided to do what she could to help other Chinese gamblers in trouble. In 2004, she started GA's first-ever weekly Chinese language meeting, to make it easier for newer immigrants and others with limited English to get help. Currently, anywhere from three to fifteen gamblers per week attend the meeting.

"I think it's been a very hard thing to keep even one Chinese GA meeting going, but it's so important," she said. "In our culture, we don't talk about problems. There's a shame to it. And that just makes troubles worse."

Asians have been the fastest-growing racial or ethnic group in America for the last decade. According to the U.S. Census Bureau, as of July 2005, 14.4 million Americans, 5 percent of the population, identified themselves as Asian or Asian "in combination with one or more other races." Between 2004 and 2005, that population grew 3 percent—faster than any other racial group in the country.

Asians are also more likely to develop significant gambling problems than any other ethnic group in American society. For a multitude of reasons, Asian Americans, including newer, often poor, and non-English speaking immigrants and refugees, are simply more at risk than other groups.

As Asian immigrants become citizens, as second- and third-generation families become rooted, gambling has remained as an integral part of many of their lives. The explanations for this include the celebration of gambling in many Asian societies; the social, family, and peer pressures to play; casinos' intensive efforts to lure Asians into their establishments; and the deep-seated, culturally based reluctance to get help when necessary.

When these factors are added together, experts say the temptation to gamble can become overwhelming.

"There's a thirst and a hunger and a demand for gambling by Asian Americans," said Timothy Fong, a psychiatrist and codirector of the UCLA Gambling Studies Program, in an interview. When addiction issues develop, he said, they're often all the more intractable. "What you get are people with problems at a much more severe level. It's often to the point where there are generational debts."

It's a phenomenon that social workers, researchers, and community activists around the country have begun to take increasingly seriously in recent years. Asian health groups for the first time are training counselors to deal with the problem. Gambling researchers are now studying the specific phenomenon of Asian problem gambling and how it differs from the broader issue among the general populace. And activists—infuriated at what they call the predatory efforts of gambling businesses to entice Asians into their establishments, and equally aggravated with politicians for legalizing gambling in their communities in the first place—are starting to fight back.

Gambling is as entrenched in the history of Asia as it is in any region of the world. Though China may have the longest gambling tradition, other East Asian cultures were never far behind, in part because of Chinese political and cultural influence in the region.

Wrote historian David Schwartz in his seminal 2006 gambling history *Roll the Bones: The History of Gambling*:

"East of India, the cultures of eastern Asia place as high a premium on gambling as any in the world. While the frequency of gambling activity in many parts of the world, including Europe and North America, was high in ancient times, East Asia had perhaps the greatest intensity of gambling, with higher stakes played for more regularly. From playing cards to keno, Asian cultures have made several important contributions to today's global culture of gambling."[1]

Gambling was well-established as a common tradition in China by the first millennium B.C. In many cities, small gambling halls thrived next to food and clothing shops. The gambling included betting on various types of animal fights.

By 200 B.C., betting on horse and dog races also became common. Several centuries later, the Chinese had adopted dice gambling, and by 900 A.D. they had invented rectangle-shaped bone tablets with numbers on them, the precursor to dominoes. Those tablets were also the basis for the game of pai gow, one of the games Angela L. played, in which players attempt to pair the tiles according to their numbers or values.

(In my hundreds of hours walking through casinos, I've seen pai gow games spread at several Las Vegas and Atlantic City casinos and southern California card rooms. Not once do I recall ever having seen a non-Asian player at a table. Likewise, the dealers at these tables are almost always Chinese-speaking. Curious about the game, with its exotic-looking shuffling rituals of slick black dominoes, I once looked at a small pai gow rules pamphlet a friendly dealer had passed to me. It was in English, but I still couldn't understand the rules when fully described; the game appeared indecipherable.)

Historians generally agree that mah-jongg likely was created in the late nineteenth century, despite the popular myth that Confucius created the game around 500 B.C.

Legal gambling in China historically has been augmented by a strong custom of underground gambling. "It's all over China," Peter

Kwong, a professor of Asian American Studies at Hunter College in New York, told me. That includes small towns, he said, where organized criminals make most of the money and enforce brutal rules. "Gambling has become a form of profit-making for some parts of the community, and oppression for others," he said.

During the pre-colonial era, gambling in Asia is thought to have been most intense in southern mainland China, Hong Kong, and Macau, and in the countries and regions directly south of China—Vietnam, Laos, Myanmar (then Burma), Thailand, and Taiwan. The Koreans invented some of their own gambling games and also adopted some invented by the Chinese, including dominoes.

In modern times, there's been a legalized gambling boom in several Asian countries. Governments strapped for cash and plagued by unemployment have been enticed by gambling in recent years, much in the same way communities in the United States have.

Though South Korea legalized casinos—for foreign gamblers only—in 1969, only in 2000 did the government allow a casino for its own citizens to be opened, the Kangwon Land casino. For years they have tried to limit the gambling of its citizens, and thus reduce the incidence of problem gambling. In 2005, the government, recognizing that many were developing addictions, took several steps to curb gambling. (One statistic had stood out: by the end of that year, the government reported that seventeen gamblers had committed suicide at the casino after losing large amounts of money.) In part this meant limiting the number of days that people could gamble per month. By 2008, exploding revenues from that casino were one cause of South Korea's National Gaming Control Commission announcing a plan to limit the total annual revenue of the gambling industry, including horse racing, lottery tickets, and casinos, to about $13.4 billion. Concerned about an increase in problem gambling behaviors, the government said it would be introducing an electronic card system that capped "excessive betting" of gamblers and tightened regulations on the entry of new players.[2]

At the same time, according to one 2009 news story, "there is increasing suspicion that the resort is becoming overzealous in exploiting losing gamblers and addicts."[3] This has led to a slew of lawsuits from addicted gamblers who say they were lured back to Kangwon Land to bet more and over the legal limit, even though they had been banned. The casino has already lost several of the suits.

Throughout the early- and mid-2000s, officials in several Japanese cities unsuccessfully lobbied for casino permits, attempting to end the country's ban on legalized casinos. Pro-gambling forces said they could create a market worth $240 billion annually. The massive gambling-machine business in Japan called pachinko already is a $232 billion industry. To put that amount in perspective, that was slightly higher than the gross domestic product of the Czech Republic for the same year. In 2008, the business drew 14.5 million Japanese through the doors of thirteen thousand pachinko halls countrywide.[4] Pachinko is legal because the government doesn't officially consider it a form of gambling. But most of the players of pachinko, sort of a hybrid between a pinball machine and a slot machine, clearly intend it as such. When they win, they can exchange the small steel balls for prizes, which in turn can easily be exchanged for money.

And though legalized gambling is banned on mainland China, it's thrived for more than a century in Hong Kong, a Chinese territory, through the Hong Kong Jockey Club (formerly known as the Royal Hong Kong Jockey Club before Britain returned Hong Kong to Chinese control). The jockey club conducts about seven hundred horse races per year at its two racetracks at Sha Tin and Happy Valley. The only other forms of legalized gambling there, including a lottery and betting on soccer matches, is also run from those two tracks.

The industry annually rakes in about $12 billion annually. The organization is the largest taxpayer in Hong Kong and the largest private donor of charity funds. About 750,000 people had telephone betting accounts as of a 2001 account—and in a city that then had a population of six million people, an astonishing one million of them, or 17 percent of the population, placed bets each race day at any of 125 off-track outlets.[5]

Here's another measure of Hong Kong's obsessive gambling intensity: the population, which as of 2010 was at seven million, is just 0.1 percent of the world's population of 6.9 billion people (as of late 2010). Yet Hong Kong makes up 3.3 percent of the world's total online gambling revenues.[6]

And then there's the modern casino mecca of Macau, which like Hong Kong is technically a special administrative region of China. In 2002, the Chinese government broke the monopoly a local casino owner named Stanley Ho held in Macau. Over the next few years, Western companies—most significantly Las Vegas–based gambling giants Wynn Resorts, MGM Mirage, and Las Vegas Sands, which runs the Venetian and Palazzo hotel/casinos in Las Vegas—flooded into the market, recognizing the gambling mania of so many in the region, and thus the massive profit potential. In 2006, Macau raked in $7 billion in casino revenue, surpassing the Las Vegas Strip as the world's biggest gambling center for the first time.

Legalized gambling on Macau has suffered since late 2008 because of the economic downturn, as well as government restrictions that prevented many Chinese citizens from the neighboring Guangdong province from visiting Macau as often as they wished. The government had grown alarmed about Guangdong residents taking too many trips there to gamble and limited their Macau visits to two per year. The government began easing those restrictions in September of 2009—an action that caused the stocks of gambling companies that do business in Macau to jump.

Las Vegas Sands, which expanded the fastest in Macau with two hotel/casinos and the Four Seasons Hotel Macao, was also hit the hardest. But they remain bullish on Macau and on the Asian gambling market generally. Sands was just one of two companies that received licenses to build mega-casinos in Singapore. The $5.4 billion Singapore resort, called the Marina Bay Sands, officially opened in April 2010. Analysts predicted it could become the world's most profitable casino. To reflect its increasing international focus, Las Vegas Sands chair and chief executive officer Sheldon Adelson said in September 2010 that the company was considering dropping the "Las Vegas" from its name. Instead, the company might change its name to Sands International or Sands Resort International, he said.[7]

In recent years, Sands has looked at building new casino resorts throughout Asia, including Japan, South Korea, Taiwan, Vietnam, and India. "We say jokingly these days that we've become an Asian company with a Las Vegas presence," said Sands vice president of communications Ron Reese in an interview a few months before the Marina Bay Sands opened its doors to the public.

Reese's business card puts the joke in stark relief. On the back side, his name, title, and business address are spelled out in Chinese characters.

As America's Asian population quickly climbs, so does its population of Asian gamblers. This has led to an increasing number of Asian problem gamblers. These are logical propositions, and several studies over the last dozen years have confirmed them. That's not to mention the anecdotes from gamblers and even casino managers, as well as simple, firsthand observation.

One of the seminal studies on gambling within Asian communities in America was released in 1997 by the NICOS Chinese Health Coalition in San Francisco. The poll, taken of about eighteen hundred members of San Francisco's Chinese American adult population, showed that they were more concerned about gambling than they were about any other issue, including health care, gangs, or crime in general. A full 70 percent of the respondents said gambling was a "problem" in their community.

"That was something that was a surprise to us—and not a surprise," said Kent Woo, NICOS's long-time executive director. Given gambling's immersion into the community, he said he had expected respondents to rank gambling as a serious concern. But not as the most serious.

After that study was released, NICOS set out to determine problem gambling rates among members of the Chinese community in San Francisco, mostly in that city's Chinatown, one of the largest Asian settlements in the western United States. The results were nothing less than remarkable.

The 1999 study,[8] which documented the behaviors of 160 Chinese-speaking adults, found that 92 percent had gambled at some point during their lifetime, including 84 percent during the last year. Of those who gambled, the study found that just 29 percent were "recreational," or so-called social gamblers. The remaining 71 percent had exhibited addictive behaviors, from the slight to the all-encompassing, including 35 percent who were deemed to be "mild" problem gamblers, 15 percent found to be problem gamblers, and a full 21 percent determined to be pathological gamblers—the most seriously addicted, who suffer a consistent failure to resist impulses to gamble, and whose chronic gambling "compromises, disrupts, or damages personal, family, or vocational pursuits."

These numbers are exponentially higher than the percentage of problem and pathological gamblers in the general population, generally considered to be between 3 and 4 percent.

A study conducted in 2002 that was led by a top problem gambling researcher in Connecticut produced results that were even more astonishing. The study researched the gambling habits of ninety southeast Asian refugees from Vietnam, Cambodia, and Laos. A full 59 percent met the criteria for being pathological gamblers.

"Extraordinarily high rates of gambling participation and problems were noted, with all but three respondents reporting gambling in their lifetimes, 95 percent having gambled in the previous year, and 93 percent having gambled in the previous two months," the researchers noted.[9] "Given that the median annual income in this sample was about $25,000, very large proportions of income were expended on gambling."

Over the last several years, Timothy Fong and his team at UCLA have conducted several studies on the topic, some of which are in progress. Much of the purpose of these studies was simply to try to determine the extent of the problem.

Fong said he started receiving a number of calls from Asian American social workers around the country in 2006, asking him for data on Asian gambling and problem gambling. He said he realized the topic needed to be studied more intensively. "We had nothing at the time," Fong said of his program. "We said, We have to do something about the issue."

In Fong's first study, conducted later that year, researchers visited a Los Angeles–area card club, with the permission of the owners, to try to substantiate a long-held hypothesis: that a large percentage of the gamblers in southern California's card rooms were of Asian descent. These card rooms, which offer legalized blackjack and pai gow poker games (pai gow poker is a card game derived from pai gow), also include several of the biggest poker rooms in the country. The researchers found that about 30 percent of the patrons were Asian or Pacific Islander. This is significantly higher than the combined population rates of those ethnic groups in California: 12 percent. What's more, researchers found that 30 percent of those Asian gamblers met the criteria for pathological gambling.

The estimations are the same all over the country, even when observations aren't backed up by scientific rigor: Asians gamble at significantly higher per capita numbers than the general population. Foxwoods, an Indian casino in Connecticut, is the largest casino in the world. It's also a major destination for Asian American gamblers. In 2006, an official there estimated that one-third or more of its forty thousand daily customers were Asian[10]—a 17 percent increase over the previous four years. This rise has been attributed to Foxwoods' persistent marketing efforts toward Asian gamblers. Its nearby rival casino, Mohegan Sun, has estimated that 20 percent of its business comes from Asian gamblers.[11] That casino has a twenty-five-person Asian American marketing department. And Asian American customers make up some 50 percent of the clientele at Pechanga Resort and Casino, a large Indian casino near the Riverside and San Diego county lines, an official there told a newspaper reporter in 2005.[12]

Overseas tourists are a big part of the ranks of these Asian gamblers. More than one in four Chinese visitors to the United States, eighty-seven thousand, included Las Vegas in their itinerary in 2006. By 2020, those numbers are expected to swell—perhaps to as many as fifteen million Chinese visitors to Las Vegas per year—as the country's middle and upper classes grow and travel restrictions are lifted.[13]

Why exactly do Asians gamble, besides the fact that many of their ancestors did so? What drew these cultures into the activity in the first place? Undoubtedly, there are many different "right" answers. And, of course, it's my aim to avoid stereotyping. Although this is obvious, it needs to be said: despite the high incidence of gambling in China and southeast Asia, there is no reason to conclude that the majority of Chinese specifically or Asians generally are problem gamblers. Yet it is the case that they are more likely to gamble—and that when they do, they're also more likely to develop problems with their gambling.

So again, why is it that so many Asians have gambled over the centuries—seemingly more than peoples of other cultures? Experts have given several reasons:

Many Chinese are fascinated by the mystical qualities of luck, fate, and chance. Gambling is a way to test that fate.

In Asian cultures, there aren't the religious prohibitions that warn against gambling as there are in several Christian denominations, Islam, and other faiths. In fact, gambling and religion in China are often part of the same general belief system. As the novelist Amy Tan wrote in *Saving Fish from Drowning*, the "Chinese kind of Buddhism" entails strong desires for riches, fame, and a large number of sons—as well as good luck at gambling.

In some Asian communities, gambling is considered a rite of passage—an activity tacitly or explicitly encouraged by parents.

Numerology is important in many Asian cultures. The numbers six and eight, for example, are considered lucky by many Chinese. Conversely, the number four, which when spoken in Cantonese and Mandarin sounds like the word for "death," is considered highly unlucky.

Finally, Asian gambling is maintained when they find their way to America because, some note, it's disproportionately risk-takers who decide to leave their safe if relatively poor existence to come to America. And many come here to get rich. Gambling is the fastest way to achieve that goal, they conclude.

Though the Chinese historically are the strongest believers in such concepts, other Asian cultures, to varying degrees, hold similar beliefs. If these beliefs fade when Asian immigrants or refugees make their way to the United States, they do so slowly. Indeed, the gambling bug appears almost as strong in second- and third-generation Asian Americans as it does in those who made the trip to America.

"Our parents gambled, and we grew up gambling, so there is no stigma attached to it," said Woo, whose parents immigrated to the United States from South China. Family members including his mother introduced him to mah-jongg when he was about ten, he recalls. They played for penny-nickel stakes, small amounts to be sure. But the gambling component of the game, as opposed to just the strategic skills utilized, added a visceral thrill. "It was never so much about money as it was about the game—though the money did make it more exciting."

According to Woo, gambling is an inextricable part of the mix of life in San Francisco's Chinatown, the largest and oldest Chinese settlement in the western United States. He estimates, for example, that there are more state lottery outlets in Chinatown per capita than anywhere else in the state. "They're sold in bakeries, dime stores, groceries. They're everywhere," he said.

Ryan Tong's father and uncle spent most of their early adult lives in the heart of that Chinatown, where his uncle ran one of dozens of illegal underground casinos that populated the neighborhood. His front business was a mah-jongg store.

As a problem gambling trainer with the Asian American Drug Abuse Program in Los Angeles, Tong, twenty-five, speaks to youth groups, seniors, and recovering drug addicts and alcoholics—anyone who will listen, really—to tell them of the dangers of gambling. He talks about the issue generally, and specifically as it applies to local Asian communities.

He said he's found the addicts to be the most receptive to his message. They are ready to hear messages about all types of addictive behaviors, even those they're not involved with, he said. But as well-ingrained as gambling is in Asian American culture and life, Tong said he's had a more difficult time reaching others in the community. "We've been in gambling a very long time. It's accepted, expected."

Tong, born in the United States, isn't much of a gambler himself. "I've always equated $5 to a sandwich as opposed to a bet," he said. But he said he's been exposed to gambling games since he was five and played mah-jongg with his grandmother, though not for money. At eight, he and his god-brother played blackjack for pocket change.

Shortly after college, Tong roomed in a big house with seven Vietnamese friends. They were "gamble-crazy," he said, and took off to Las Vegas whenever they could. He generally avoided the trips.

When his current job with the drug abuse program came open, Tong, then a youth counselor, said he was reluctant to sign up. His mostly secondhand experiences with gambling didn't lead him to believe that it was such a big problem. He said he took the job to develop skills as a trainer, rather than because of the mission itself.

That's changed. Said Tong: "Once I got into the work and the data, and started seeing my family and my community in the data, I said, 'Now this *is* all about me.'"

Gambling operators—especially the casino business—have for decades been aware of the value of building a strong base of Asian gamblers. In recent years, those efforts have influenced the way casinos are designed and which games are offered; spurred casinos to send fleets of buses to any nearby Chinatown to shuttle Asian gamblers to the casino; sparked the creation of special Asian-themed high-roller "clubs" with private gambling and dining rooms; and even caused more than one Las Vegas mega-casino to avoid calling the fourth and fortieth hotel floors as such because of the negative connotation of the number four in Chinese.

Caesars Palace in Las Vegas was among the first to recognize the potential of the Asian gambler. In the 1970s, the casino was the first to launch an Asian marketing department. In 1975, the casino celebrated the Chinese New Year—something that's now done at casinos across the country.

In 2006, the Showboat Casino in Atlantic City unveiled a gambling and dining area utilizing architectural elements from the Chinese Ming and Song dynasties, including importing carved woods from China to house baccarat and pai gow poker tables. Harrah's Entertainment chair and CEO Gary Loveman bragged at the time that it was "the country's first authentic Asian gaming pit."

The following year, table game revenue from the Showboat increased 35 percent to $63 million. The casino had more than doubled its business from Asian players. Loveman next experimented with a similar Asian gambling pit at Caesars Atlantic City, with similar results. That spurred him to order such additions at Harrah's casinos across the country. He phrased it pithily to the *New York Times*: "There's this interest in gambling among the Chinese that transcends anything you see in any other socioeconomic or ethnic group."[14]

Asian gambling pits are now ubiquitous, as are increased Asian dining options at almost all midsize and large casinos. Casinos regularly are utilizing the services of feng shui masters when designing such areas—or for that matter, entire casinos. This wasn't the case in 1993, when the MGM Grand opened in Las Vegas. To use the main entrance, patrons had to walk through the open mouth of a huge lion, MGM's iconic corporate symbol. But Asian gamblers, who felt it bad luck to walk into the mouth of a beast, stayed away in droves. MGM spent millions to reconfigure the entrance.

If you're sensitive to it, it's now almost impossible to walk into most new casinos and not feel the Asian design influences. Wynn Las Vegas and Encore, Wynn's newer sister property next-door, may be the clearest examples, from the use of curved walkways and circular entryways to the use of red, the luckiest of colors among the Chinese. Encore's casino floor, with its thick greenery, butterfly motif, and insistent reds, including scores of low-hanging, brilliant ruby-red Rubino chandeliers, is as feng shui–centered—as catered to Chinese notions of good luck and health—as seems possible.

These are just some of the ways casinos are trying to lure Asians into their establishments. There are many others. As of 2004, for example, Indian casinos outside Seattle hosted Asian-themed holiday celebrations, including events for Chinese New Year and the Vietnamese Lunar New Year. They brought in top-flight Asian popular musical acts and boasted Asian restaurants, including sushi and Vietnamese noodle bars. Casino newspaper and television advertisements often prominently featured Asian dealers and Asian actors playing gamblers.

Casinos have also taken to hiring large numbers of Asian employees to assist Asian customers, and to make comfortable those whose English is limited or nonexistent. Nearly one in seven employees at Mohegan Sun is Asian American, for example; at Foxwoods the number is one in six.[15]

Every day, from Seattle to Boston, casinos are sending a constant stream of buses to Asian neighborhoods to get favored customers—who include large numbers of elderly gamblers on fixed incomes—inside their doors. As many as eighty buses per day stop in San Francisco's Chinatown to take gamblers to nearby Indian casinos. In Boston, as many as fifty buses per day pick up mostly Asian gamblers to take them to Foxwoods and the Mohegan Sun in Connecticut. In New York, the buses headed for the Connecticut casinos, as well as several in Atlantic City, pick up gamblers in each of the largest Asian neighborhoods several times per day, including in Manhattan's Chinatown; Flushing, Queens; and Sunset Park in Brooklyn. For Foxwoods alone, the promotional bus trips bring in 750,000 Asian patrons per year.[16]

These buses are often free for the gambler or cost very little. The casinos also usually provide modest betting vouchers and a free lunch. And some gamblers say they welcome the buses; the casino visits serve as their chief form of entertainment.

The most apparent danger of these buses was illustrated in October of 2008 when forty-three southeast Asians, most of whom were elderly, boarded a bus in Sacramento. The bus was headed for the Colusa Casino Resort when it flipped over. Ten passengers died as a result.

Helen Gym said she's had enough. Gym, a community activist with a group called Asian Americans United, was on the forefront of the effort to keep Foxwoods from locating a casino about a block from Philadelphia's Chinatown. This proposed casino was a result of the law Pennsylvania passed several years ago to allow new casinos to be opened with thousands of slot machines. Ever since, there have been debates about exactly where they should go. Gym—the *Philadelphia Inquirer*'s 2007 Citizen of the Year—and scores of others fought the proposed site tooth and nail, and they won when Foxwoods backed down and selected another downtown Philadelphia location.

Gym said in an interview that Foxwoods' effort reflected the rapacious practices of casinos and other gambling purveyors that are increasingly targeting Asians, regardless of the costs to the gamblers, their families, or the communities. The casino buses, she said, are turning valued members of Asian communities into absentees.

The time is long past due, Gym said, for a national dialogue within the Asian community about how to address the issue. She said she's primed to lead it.

"This marketing goes beyond targeting and into predatory practices," she said. "We consider it to be a devastating thing."

As might be expected, casino companies hotly deny their practices are predatory. Alan Feldman, senior vice president of public affairs for MGM Mirage, declined to talk directly about his company's marketing practices, but he said that once Asian gamblers were in the doors of an MGM property, they were treated like any other gamblers. "The policies and practices to reduce problem gambling in our casinos obviously applies across the board, and not just to any one group." When a gambler is exhibiting behaviors leading a dealer to believe they have a problem, "we encourage people to take a break, regardless of their ethnicity."

On this issue, Fong of UCLA comes to the casino industry's defense. He notes casinos' "aggressive" marketing efforts toward Asians and said that when he first saw the Chinatown buses, he said to himself, "Gosh, that just doesn't seem right." And yet, regarding casinos' marketing efforts toward Asians generally, "I don't see that as morally or ethically wrong. They go after Asians because of their market share."

To be sure, Fong said, both the casino business and local and state governments could do more to help Asian gamblers who develop problems. For starters, politicians need to be more careful when deciding whether to approve new legalized gambling in a community, and need to do more to provide assistance to those who develop problems. He had other specific recommendations. The state should disallow payday loan operations within casinos, which cater to addicted gamblers. Casinos should offer on-site counselors specifically trained to assist Asian problem gamblers. And Asian American community groups need to do more to develop alternative types of entertainment, he said, so that casinos don't hold as much appeal.

I could understand the appeal from the swank confines of the exclusive high-roller club on the fiftieth floor of the Palazzo, one of the newest and most luxurious Las Vegas Strip hotels. I was there visiting the Paiza Club with Reese, the Las Vegas Sands vice president. He says the Paiza Clubs are the company's high-end "international gaming brand." There are clubs like this on the top floor of the Venetian next door and in the Sands casinos in Macau.

The view is stunning from Palazzo's top-floor club, one of the highest vantage points on the Strip. But it's the interior that's most interesting. It's as though the rarefied few who gamble at high enough levels to use the club—an "overwhelming" number of whom are Asian, said Reese—are back in China. There are Chinese newspapers strewn about, and all but one of the televisions are turned to a Chinese-language station. The decor is plush and Asian-accented, and the attentive staff is entirely Asian, at least on the day I visit. At one end of the room are several dining tables. Reese says those tables, and the club's chefs who are on call twenty-four hours a day, allow travelers to order dim sum or any other food they like, at any time. On the other side of the room, the club also has small private gaming salons for those who like to wager in quieter surroundings. Because these tables aren't open to the general public, the cameras overseeing the action feed directly to Nevada's Gaming Control Board.

The Asian theme makes sense, given that 80 to 90 percent of the biggest bettors, or "whales" in gambling parlance, are from places like Hong Kong, Shanghai, Seoul, and Tokyo. According to Reese, Sands' Las Vegas casinos took on more Asian accents as it opened its Macau properties, for purposes of "cross-pollination." We toured one such series of gambling rooms at the Venetian, remodeled in 2004, off of the main gambling floor. One of the rooms, a lounge, boasted a large and ornate black cabinet lined with brightly colored Chinese tea vases.

Reese rejected the notion that Asian cultures were in any way being exploited by these efforts. "We're hypersensitive to not doing that," he said. "I think the fact that you look at a place like this—we've spent multimillions developing a product here that would feel comfortable to Asian customers. I think you're the furthest thing away from exploitation when you look at it as a way where you can provide a service that people are really going to appreciate."

Ultimately, Reese said, Americans view gaming differently than Asians. "I think Asians view it as destiny, challenging luck. Americans view it as, you know, part of the entertainment, part of the overall experience," he said. "So for example, here in Las Vegas, look at this town. You've got billions invested in properties that have celebrity chef restaurants, Broadway shows, outrageous nightclubs. Vegas has evolved to the point to where a property like the Venetian, two-thirds of our revenue comes from non-gaming. That's going to be really difficult at any point to ever happen in an Asian operation."

In the end, say Asian American health experts and social workers, it's not the whales who are most at risk. It's those who truly can't afford to lose the money they gamble. Government has failed, they say, in providing the necessary means both to prevent Asian gamblers from developing problems, and then treating them when this does happen. Nonprofits are filling the breach.

Woo said that his group's 1997 study spurred the creation of the Chinese Community Task Force on Gambling the following year. The task force and a resulting problem gambling project since have enrolled more than two hundred local clinicians in problem gambling counseling training. They've also developed a public education campaign including Chinese-language problem gambling literature and set up a toll-free hotline to assist problem gamblers.

Dr. Eddie Chiu has been treating Chinese-speaking problem gamblers in the San Francisco area since 1999. As director of the Asian Family Institute within the social services group Richmond Area Multi-Services, Chiu, a psychologist, said his services have filled a strong need. Historically, Asians who develop gambling problems have both been overrepresented among the general problem gambling community and underserved.

In addition to holding sessions with individual gamblers, Chiu, who immigrated to the United States from Hong Kong in 1991, now leads a regular Chinese-language problem gambling therapy group in San Francisco's Richmond District. Chiu said he's treated hundreds of patients—a wide range, from low-income workers and newly arrived immigrants to members of some of the city's wealthiest families.

"For me, it's not easy. It's a trick compared with other mental disorders," said Chiu, fifty. Failing at gambling and developing mental health issues because of it, then seeking help from outsiders, is often seen as disgraceful. Chiu said in the last several years since a toll-free telephone help line for Chinese-speaking problem gamblers was set up, the types of people who call it has changed. At first, only family members or close friends of problem gamblers would call. Now, after years of targeted outreach through paid advertising and occasional news stories, including some in Chinese publications, gamblers themselves are calling. But the numbers of those who phone in annually—somewhere north of two hundred, Chiu estimated—pales in comparison with the tens of thousands of gamblers who need help.

Harumi Hashimoto, a problem gambling counselor with the Asian Counseling and Referral Service in Seattle, made a related point. It can be seen as a battle for the hearts and minds of Asian gamblers—and the casinos, card rooms, and horse tracks have a big edge. "Because of language or cultural barriers, they often struggle to communicate or connect with others," she said in a written re-

sponse to questions. Gambling provides Asian immigrants and refugees with limited English a familiar and welcoming environment,
even if ultimately it's a destructive environment for many of them.

Hashimoto said it stands to reason that the more gamblers find
themselves inside a casino, the more likely it is they will find themselves battling a burgeoning addiction. And the hills those gamblers
have to climb to get out of trouble are often steeper for Asians. "Ad-
mitting an addiction is difficult in any culture. But many Asians find
it particularly challenging, especially men," she said. "It's shameful to
be emotionally weak. Besides, we don't have a help-seeking culture.
Professional counseling and psychotherapy still bear a negative image.
And even those who recognize they need help may have difficulty
finding it due to limited access to services or language barriers."

Of all the stories I heard from the experts, activists, and counselors,
Peter Yee's may be the most instructive. As a top official with the
biggest social services agency focusing on New York's Asian population, he has set up a thriving counseling program for Asian problem
gamblers.

He's also an avid, unapologetic gambler. His own gambling,
which he says has never become problematic, has nonetheless
helped inform his mission to help others. "I've seen human suffering
and tragedy," he says.

Yee, fifty-two, was born in Hong Kong and moved to Boston in
1966. He's still close with his old buddies there. As kids and teens,
he and his friends loved to gamble. They used to go bowling and play
the basketball game called HORSE for money. One of his friends
got into so much trouble with a bookie that he escaped by joining the
Coast Guard when he was eighteen.

As a social worker, Yee has served as the assistant executive director for behavioral health services at the Hamilton Madison House,
headquartered in the Two Bridges neighborhood of Manhattan's
Lower East Side, near Chinatown, for the last eight years. Recogniz-

ing the need to develop a problem gambling treatment program, he said the first step was to train his counselors. He sent a case manager to Hong Kong and Macau to receive specialized training. In turn, that manager trained several others. Yee said he now has five counselors treating twenty-six problem gamblers. Most of his agency's gambling clients are Chinese; a couple are Korean. All are recent immigrants to the United States who developed big gambling problems, fast. He said he understands how their problems were formed.

"This is an outlet for them," said Yee, who also serves as president of the New York Coalition for Asian American Mental Health. Many Asians' lives are "very regimented; there's no risk involved. Gambling allows for risk-taking. It provides heightened excitement."

He also notes how Asian gamblers have been glorified through the proliferation of televised poker tournaments. "It's probably the highest representation of Asians in sports, by far," he said. "It's part of our culture."

Yee classified himself as a recreational gambler. He takes his family to Las Vegas two to three times a year, and he said they love the trips. He noted that his family vacations aren't centered only around gambling. They also go on skiing trips and take in sporting events. But clearly gambling is an outlet Yee relishes. In addition to the Vegas trips, he also visits the Mohegan Sun casino in Connecticut two or three times per year, alone. He used to play blackjack, he said, but switched to pai gow poker.

"I look at this . . . I set aside money for this," he said. And if he loses his gambling bankroll, he stops. "For me, I like the rush. Winning and losing is secondary to the rush of chance."

Yee says his family hasn't been impacted adversely by his gambling. Laura Chen can only wish that was the case with hers.

As a child growing up in New York, family trips to Atlantic City were a big part of Chen's life. No other place, in fact, became as important to her family. Chen's parents, Vietnamese refugees who owned a Brooklyn nail salon, led visits down to the Trump Taj Mahal casino as many as eight times a year. Sometimes with a large extended family in tow, Chen and her older sister were told that the main purpose of the trips were the Chinese or Vietnamese pop concerts the big boardwalk casinos were holding as a draw for Asian gamblers. (Chen agreed to be interviewed only on condition that her real name not be used.)

This went on for about a half-dozen years in the early and mid-1990s, when Chen was between six and twelve years old. For the children, the excursions usually were boring. While Chen's parents gambled, she and her sister often were left alone for hours at a stretch to hang out in their room, at a children's arcade, or on the boardwalk. Her sister, who is six years older, would watch over her. Other times an aunt who didn't like to gamble much would babysit both of them. Chen's mom almost never ate with the children because she was gambling, "sometimes for days on end," Chen said. The family's stay was usually comped by the hotel, she later learned, because of the high amounts her mom gambled and usually lost at the casino's baccarat tables.

Chen, now a graduate student at UCLA, said her parents would find any pretext to shut down their salon and make the two-and-a-half-hour jaunt to the dingy coastal casino town. They took off during several Jewish holidays despite the fact that Chen's family isn't Jewish and almost none of their salon's customers were. They even took off for Groundhog Day. "It didn't matter," she said, laughing. "Any excuse to close the shop and off we'd go."

For years, Chen didn't know what those trips were really about— or that her parents, especially her mother, were engaging in activity they didn't want the kids to know about.

Chen's mother grew up as a poor child from an ethnically Chinese family in Saigon (known as Ho Chi Minh City since 1976)— and she grew up gambling. She started at nine, gambling with her family and neighbors. Later, as so many around her did, she went to bars and clubs to gamble. Chen's parents emigrated from southern

Vietnam to Hawaii in 1979. Her mother was twenty-one; her father about two decades older. From there they moved to Los Angeles and then to New York in 1985, the year Chen was born. They moved back to Los Angeles several years ago, while Chen was in high school. Her parents now own and operate a restaurant there.

For the first few years back in Los Angeles, Chen said gambling was her mother's main preoccupation. She told her daughter at one point that she wanted to become a professional gambler. One time, Chen said after her mother returned from a nearby Indian casino having won $40,000, she bought Chen's older sister a used Mercedes. She paid with cash. But the big win was an aberration. In the larger sense, she was steadily losing the family's hard-earned money. The family had made hundreds of thousands of dollars through their nail salon in New York, but that nest egg was being put at risk. The family's stocks were sold, their savings accounts bled dry.

Chen said her father would often join her mother on her gambling trips. They would go to Las Vegas, or more often to the large Indian casinos spread throughout southern California. In part, he would go to play his favorite game, pai gow poker. But he knew how to set limits, Chen said. If he planned to lose no more than $1,000, he would stop if he lost that much. The main reason her father went on those trips was so that he could reign in his wife if she lost too much or stayed too long—and simply could not leave on her own. "My dad said, 'I need to control her,'" Chen said.

As high school turned into college and then grad school—all of which were near her parents, unlike her older sister, who works in New York—Chen became increasingly concerned about her mother's gambling. When she took weekend trips home to visit her parents, her mother often was absent. At one point, Chen downloaded and printed out a Gamblers Anonymous pamphlet and taped torn pages on her parent's bathroom and bedroom walls. Her mother ripped them down, angrily telling Chen that she didn't have a problem.

Chen's family's problems hit new lows after her parents purchased a restaurant in early 2008. Initially, Chen said her mother put all of her energies into the restaurant and her gambling diminished. Yet Chen said she believes the toll of her mother's gambling, and the constant stresses of the floundering new business, which initially lost as much as $20,000 per month, were factors behind her father's suicide attempt in June of that year.

Her parents persevered, largely without gambling, until March of 2009, when Chen's mother, who is in her mid-fifties, hit a new bottom. That month, a friend of Chen's mother convinced her to drive the two of them to an Indian casino, the Pechanga Resort and Casino in Temecula, California, to take a break from the restaurant pressures. She ended up staying for three days, long after she sent her friend back to Los Angeles on a bus. When Chen heard about her mother's return to the casino—and the fact that she refused to leave when her friend wanted them both to go—it terrified her. Her fears were confirmed when her mother called three days after arriving at the casino, on a Saturday morning, crying. Her mother never cried. She was badly in the hole. After losing an initial $1,000, Chen said, casino officials allowed her mother to take a marker out for another $35,000—and she'd lost most of that.

Chen rushed to the casino to try to rescue her. She hurried into the high-limit area, where the biggest baccarat games were found. For the first time, she noted that the exclusive den seemed to be filled only with Chinese, Korean, and Vietnamese gamblers. She found her mother, rooted to a table and looking bedraggled. Though the casino had comped her mother a room, it appeared that she hadn't slept much, if at all. By the time Chen had found her, she was almost down to the felt. Chen took her mother aside and begged her to stop. Her mother resisted, saying she needed to win back her losses. "You've got to let me play," her mother told her. "If I don't play, I'll die."

Chen convinced her mother to leave. And eventually, to get help. They found a Chinese language Gamblers Anonymous meeting— the one started by Angela L.—in Hacienda Heights. There were language barriers for her mother, who reads Vietnamese but not Chinese. Most of the recovering gamblers, including her mother, were able to successfully communicate through a combination of Cantonese, Mandarin, and English. Her mother went to two more meetings on her own but then dropped out.

Chen said her mom's gambling has recently slowed, mostly by necessity. With the exception of the modest cash flow coming into the restaurant, her parents are out of money. Chen and her sister are doing what they can to support them. It's a strain, but it is necessary. "My sister takes care of them financially," she said. "I take care of them every other way. I help out at the restaurant and at home. And I try to keep my mom away from the casino."

A brief postscript: I touched base with Chen again in October 2010, about one year after I initially spoke with her to hear her family's story. I was curious to see if there had been any big developments.

The good news was that her mother stopped gambling after what Chen termed "the last big scare" involving the trip to the Pechanga Resort and Casino. Chen said in an e-mail that while she constantly fears a relapse, her mother's newfound ability to abstain from gambling has helped both her parents regain a sense of normalcy. "Fortunately, their mental health is a lot better," she wrote.

But some of the gambling-related damage caused by her mother apparently could not be undone. Her parents' depleted financial situation resulted in a distressing development: they're moving a continent away from their two daughters. Her parents have decided to return to Vietnam, where the significantly lower cost of living will allow them to live without as many financial stresses.

Chen wrote that other Asian American families are quietly suffering similar fates, especially as legalized gambling is increasingly within reach of more communities. She was grateful to be able to tell her family's tale. "Thank you for publishing our story," she wrote. "The Asian-American gambling experience is one that needs to be more widely shared."

CHAPTER 4

The Rise of the Poker Junkie

It was typical autumn weather in Seattle, cold and wet, the night I first drove south on Interstate 5 to Diamond Lil's Card Casino, one of the better-known poker rooms in the area. The sparsely decorated room boasted nine poker tables and large, beer company–sponsored posters of playing card kings, queens, and jacks on the walls, and it was buzzing with the clattering of clay chips. The smells of deep-fried foods wafted into the gambling pit from the adjacent bar. Most of the players waiting for a seat milled about the tables, staring intently at the games, their eyes heavy with anticipation.

I made the trip in late 2000, a few years before the national poker boom began in earnest. As I sat down to play at a $4–$8 Texas Hold'em cash game, I fumbled with my chips and had little idea when or how to bet. I quickly lost my buy-in of $100 and bolted.

Upset as I was at my first night at Lil's—my second time ever playing in a poker room as opposed to a more casual home game—I was taken in by the sordid atmosphere, the heady rush of the action. I couldn't believe how much fun casino poker was, and not just the adrenalized gambling. There were cerebral challenges involving psychology and advanced math. And then there were more subtle skills to be learned. Mystical, sixth-sense abilities. Like being able to silently manipulate opponents into doing precisely what you want them to do. Or being able to read other players' hands, to know to a dead certainty what cards they're holding.

Poker players bristle at being labeled, derisively or dismissively, as gamblers. As though our game—where learned and innate skills play crucial parts, where the ability to observe and conceal can mean the world or nothing on any given hand—has much to do with slots or craps or roulette, unbeatable games driven entirely by luck.

It didn't take me long to get back to Lil's, and eventually to more than a dozen poker rooms and Indian casinos in the Seattle area. I immersed myself in the region's poker subculture slowly at first, mostly playing small tournaments—meaning events that typically cost less than $100 to enter. As I became increasingly comfortable, I played more in cash games. Unlike tournaments, in which you buy in for a set amount and only play until you lose all your chips or win everyone else's, cash or "ring" games have no cost- or time-limits. At first, I played mainly on the weekends. Later, I started playing weeknights as well. Sometimes I won. But often I played until I lost everything I had in my pocket, or more after a short walk to an ATM.

Over the course of the last decade, as legalized gambling has spread around the country and the poker business has concurrently boomed, I've raised, called, and folded everywhere from the giant poker warehouses of southern California to card rooms in the Mississippi Delta and on Kansas City riverboats.

To date, I know I've lost far more than I've won. I've never determined the exact amount. Yet my game has improved. Though I still often lack the discipline needed to be a winning cash game player, I have become a relatively skillful and consistent poker tournament player. In 2007 and 2008, I earned about $60,000 in nine tournaments big enough to be recognized by CardPlayer.com, one of the poker industry's main websites. Both years, for what it's worth, I was ranked by the site to be among the top 4,100 poker tournament players in the world.

But here's the thing: having some ability hasn't saved me from developing a damaging habit. This is the case with lots of poker players. There is no correlation between a poker player's ability and the likelihood that the player might also develop a gambling dependency. I've known low-limit players with few skills who, after losing their $50 weekly gambling allowance, happily and easily walked away from the game—and other bad players who regularly lost and then tapped out their bank accounts before begging other players to put them back in the game. At the same time, there are a small number of highly skilled poker professionals who win consistently, treat their poker like a business, manage their money professionally, and don't otherwise gamble or engage in potentially addictive behaviors—and many more who exhibit the classic signs of addiction.

Gambling treatment experts have concluded that becoming good at poker—leading many to believe they can "beat the game" over the long haul—often makes it more difficult for players to concede they've developed a destructive addiction and harder for them to be successfully treated.

This was the case with Frank, who had embedded himself in the thick of the high-stakes poker boom of the last decade.

In a telephone interview, Frank spoke quickly—sometimes so fast that it made it difficult to get in another question—and only on condition that he not be identified by his real name. He said that he loved to gamble since he was a kid growing up in New England. That culminated when he was in high school and tried to sneak into a nearby Indian casino but was kicked out for being underage. He continued gambling after being accepted into an Ivy League university in the early 1990s, when he and his friends took weekend road trips to a different Indian casino that allowed gamblers as young as eighteen. They sometimes played for thirty-six hours at a stretch, he said, before heading back to their dorm.

Frank, now in his mid-thirties, also used his time in college to begin building a small but successful business, which continued to grow after he left college before graduating. He sold the company in 1999 for a seven-figure amount. The next year, he began gambling in earnest. Specifically, he sharpened his skills at poker and began mostly winning, he said. He also picked up an online poker habit. After the World Poker Tour began sponsoring an annual series of large tournaments in late 2002, he started following the circuit to different casinos around the country. For months at a stretch, he lived in luxurious gambling resorts like Bellagio and the Mirage in Las Vegas.

Before long, Frank also began playing blackjack, especially after losing poker sessions. He lost badly—far more than he ever won at the poker tables, in part by accepting large sums in credit, called markers, the casinos were willing to give him. And he was living a crazed gambling lifestyle that was burning him out. He recalled one early-morning no-limit Texas Hold'em cash game at Wynn Las Vegas, soon after the casino/hotel opened in 2005. He and several others bet thousands on whether a filet mignon-and-eggs breakfast would cost over or under $42. Players made bets like that—called proposition or "prop bets"—all the time, he said.

As his bankroll dried up and his unpaid gambling markers mounted, Frank's family intervened and he quit. He's still paying down a large marker to a prominent Las Vegas Strip casino he asked not be named. When I spoke with him in June 2010, he said he was coming up on four years in Gamblers Anonymous, without placing a bet. He had gained a different perspective on his old gambling friends, many of whom have been promoted by websites, magazines, and TV shows as poker superstars to be admired and emulated.

"Ninety-plus percent of them are compulsive gamblers," he said. "They gamble on everything to stay in action. You can't really call yourself a professional gambler without being a compulsive gambler."

Frank's step toward recovery and away from a poker and gambling life—"it had beaten me mentally, physically, emotionally"—is mirroring that of a growing number of poker players.

•   •   •

The game has a rich and broad history in America. It's chock-full of archetypal characters, from heavy drinking Old West gunmen shot dead while playing in saloons, to paranoid future presidents raking in huge pots from wartime buddies.

As poker writer and player James McManus noted in *Cowboys Full: The Story of Poker,* the game's rise was hastened by the nation's push westward toward the Pacific. President Jefferson's Louisiana Purchase and the subsequent winning of the Battle of New Orleans—the home of poker's antecedent game, called "poque" and later "pokuh" after arriving on southern American shores—laid the groundwork for the game's spread north and west.

"The entire length of the continent, [Jefferson] believed, would now be settled by one people 'speaking the same language, governed in similar forms, and by similar laws,'" McManus wrote. "What he did not say was how natural it would be for such a people to share a taste for a new kind of card game, one whose rules favored a frontiersman's initiative and cunning, an entrepreneur's creative sense of risk, and a democratic openness to every class of player."

By 2001, it was estimated that forty-five million Americans played poker on a regular basis.[1] And that was before the boom. In the following five years, poker exploded. There were three main reasons given for this: the advent of online poker, which was drawing a new generation of players both to virtual and actual poker tables; the "hole camera" technology used by the World Poker Tour and other poker television shows, which allowed American viewers for the first time to see the cards players were raising or folding with and made TV poker a viable entertainment even for non-players; and the success of "everyman" Chris Moneymaker, the appropriately named Tennessee accountant who beat the pros to win the 2003 World Series of Poker main event.

The rest of the world has followed suit. In 2001, players paid $72 million for live poker tournament buy-ins.[2] That worldwide number rose to $390 million in 2005, and peaked at just over $700 million in 2008.[3] As the economic downturn took hold, the number dipped in 2009, to $575 million.[4] At the same time, the number of people entering those tournaments worldwide has risen sharply. In 2001, about 147,000 players entered poker tournaments.[5] By 2008, that number more than tripled to 515,000.[6]

Other data bolster the notion that there is now a substantially higher number of Americans playing poker than there were before the boom hit earlier in the decade.

Subscriptions to *Card Player* magazine, one of the leading magazines covering the poker business, shot up tenfold from 2001 to 2005, from three thousand to thirty thousand.[7] And poker has exploded on television, drawing more fans and new players than ever to the game. As of the mid-1990s, a single network broadcast just one hour-long poker show per year on TV. By contrast, during one week in mid-2010, fifty-eight episodes of fourteen different poker tournaments or cash games ran on eight different networks.[8]

Another way to gauge this is to look at the number of entrants into the $10,000 buy-in main event of the World Series of Poker in Las Vegas, historically considered the most prestigious annual poker tournament, and the one with the richest payouts. In 1990, a paltry 194 people entered. A decade later, there were 512. Ten years after that, in 2010, an incredible 7,319 people signed up for the event. Apart from the 2006 tournament, that was the highest number of entrants ever for the main event. Moreover, the entire six-week 2010 World Series, composed of fifty-seven different tourneys, boasted a record number of players, about seventy-three thousand, and the biggest overall prize pool in its history, more than $187 million.[9]

And none of this is to mention the number of Americans who play online poker for money (which I delve into more thoroughly in the next chapter)—ten million, according to one 2009 survey. That number is more than five times as large as the country with the next-highest number of online players, the United Kingdom.[10]

•   •   •

Live poker rooms of various sorts—inside Indian and commercial casinos and smaller card rooms—are legal in about half of the states. In 2006, *Card Player* magazine estimated there were about 4,200 poker tables in four hundred different poker rooms in the United States. Almost half of those tables, 1,900, were in California and Nevada.[11] And the nationwide numbers are growing. In mid-2010, table games including poker were allowed into casinos for the first time in Delaware and Pennsylvania. At the same time, more than two decades after the state legislature in Florida allowed small-stakes Texas Hold'em games to operate, the government allowed for a significant expansion of its casinos' poker games. It scrapped the $100 limit buy-in for cash games, making the game truly no limit, and expanded the hours that poker rooms can operate to practically 24–7. The change likely will have a major impact on the state's twenty-three poker rooms that are attached to horse and dog racing tracks and jai alai frontons, and the seven rooms inside Indian casinos. Industry analysts predicted the move could propel southern Florida into one of the top poker destinations in the country alongside Las Vegas and southern California.[12]

Moreover, poker has belatedly taken off in Europe and elsewhere around the world—a trend that symbiotically aids the national poker scene through increased international participation in U.S.–based tournaments. From 2005 to 2010, poker cash games and tournament series have proliferated throughout Europe, and to a lesser extent also in Australia, New Zealand, South America, and in parts of Asia, including China's Macau and South Korea.

Several years after the poker boom began, some media accounts took note of the fact that the numbers, from tournament registrations to viewership of TV poker shows, were dropping. They concluded that the trend had worn itself out. "Three years into the poker boom, the game's purveyors are out to prove that it is not a mere fad, but a form of entertainment with real legs—even as there are signs that the country's poker appetite may be becoming less ravenous. Some industry analysts expect the growth of online poker to slow sharply, and televised poker is already drawing fewer viewers," concluded a 2006 *New York Times* story.[13]

It is true that in the United States poker's popularity may have peaked in 2005 and 2006. But if so, the fade has been molasses-slow. I would submit that poker's future remains rosy. Here are four reasons why: First, the gambling industry's unrelenting push for growth often has included the legalization of poker rooms as a component. Second, the rise of international poker only aids the U.S. industry. Third, the 2006 law called Unlawful Internet Gambling Enforcement Act (UIGEA), which scared many Americans from becoming online poker players—and by extent, some believe, dampened the live poker scene in this country—soon could be overturned by Congress. Finally, poker's popularity with the millions of folks who play in regular home games with family, friends, and colleagues hasn't diminished. They'll continue to be among those ready to take advantage of newly opened poker rooms that may sprout up closer to where they live.

As an enduring pop-culture phenomenon and American leisure activity, it seems poker is here to stay.

Poker's explosive rise has added to the overall number of problem gamblers in this country, treatment workers and other experts submit. This reality isn't just exemplified by numerous newspapers stories of college students and other young players who followed the national gambling trend of the mid-2000s, picked up the game, and then developed problems with it—though there are a number of these gamblers out there. Poker also has become a refuge for gamblers of all ages to grow and feed their general gambling addictions, as was the case with Frank. Because better players can make their bankrolls last longer, poker rooms have become havens for addicted gamblers to exercise their jones with more of a sense of safety.

"When they put the TV shows on, they changed the perception of poker, they turned it into a sport," said Arnie Wexler, the former executive director of the Council on Compulsive Gambling of New Jersey. "This has caused big problems."

Wexler, who runs a toll-free telephone hotline for gamblers in need of help, said in an interview that about a third of the calls he receives these days are from poker players, many of whom are younger than thirty. When they begin playing, these young players don't look at its addictive potential. "These people all think they're professionals, and the colleges don't educate the kids to tell them of the pitfalls associated with gambling. Nobody gets this," he said.

Heiko Ganzer has been in the problem gambling treatment business since 1993, when he started the first program on Long Island. Ganzer, the former president of the New York Council on Problem Gambling, runs Money Addictions of America, which treats not just gambling addicts (75 percent of the group's business), but also those who develop troubles with spending, shopping, credit card debt, and Internet use.

Among the problem gamblers he sees, poker players "have certainly grown a substantial amount" in recent years, Ganzer said in a telephone chat. "The young folks in college, that's what they do. They play poker at their college or they go to casinos. Gambling is a rite of passage for them, the way cigarettes or sex or drugs used to be. It's exciting."

Poker's reliance on gamblers' abilities often gets in the way when they decide they've had enough, Ganzer said. "They're more convinced by their periodic winning that they have a skill than, say, a horse player or a lottery player. They're harder to treat because of that," he said.

By 2004, poker had become a "wildly contagious teen craze," according to a *Philadelphia Inquirer* story.[14] Studies were released that reinforced the notion. In 2005, an estimated 2.9 million teens and young adults from fourteen to twenty-two years old were estimated to be playing "card gambling" games—by and large meaning poker—on a monthly basis. That included a 20 percent rise from the year before among teen boys and young men, according to the survey from the Annenberg Public Policy Center.[15] The same report found that just over half of those who gambled weekly reported at least one symptom of problem gambling, including preoccupation with gambling or "overspending" on it. "Card players tend to report more problem gambling symptoms than other types of weekly gamblers. If the trend toward card playing among young people continues, the overall severity of symptoms may also continue to increase," the report found.

The teen poker craze died down somewhat in the years following that report. A follow-up study from Annenberg three years later found that monthly gambling on cards by young males had dropped by about 30 percent. It was noted that during that same time frame, there were concurrent rises in sports betting and other forms of gambling.[16]

Over the last several years, a number of wild stories seeped into the press regarding poker players resorting to criminal acts to fund their casino and online poker habits. In 2007, for example, Joe Watson, a former newspaper and magazine journalist, was arrested after committing a string of more than a half-dozen robberies of tanning salons and other small businesses in Scottsdale, Arizona. Watson, nicknamed the Salon Bandit, told police he committed the crimes to support his gambling addiction. According to a report from one his former employers, the alternative weekly newspaper *Phoenix New Times*, he was arrested by Scottsdale detectives while "doing one of his favorite things—playing poker at Casino Arizona." He didn't resist arrest.[17]

·   ·   ·

Top poker players recognize the addictive allure of the game. Often, they defuse the touchy subject by joking about it. Just as often, they're not kidding around. Many of poker's all-time greats, including several ensconced in the Poker Hall of Fame in Las Vegas— clearly also were or are gambling addicts. By his own words, that would appear to include Doyle Brunson, the high-stakes cash game and tournament professional, author, operator of the DoylesRoom .com poker website, and legendary Texas roadhouse gambler. He's the most revered player in the game, and one of the best-recognized and liked with his trademark Stetson and outgoing, good-natured personality. Brunson writes a blog on his DoylesRoom website, which includes a "Doyleism of the Day" that begins with witticisms such as: "It's far easier to forgive an enemy after you've gotten even with him." Even as he serves unofficially as poker's most prominent ambassador, Brunson has referred to the potential pitfalls of poker as a lifestyle. He was bracingly honest about his career choice in a May 16, 2010, blog post on his website:

> Damn! Just when I was feeling good and had decided to make a full-blown run trying to win a bracelet at the [World Series of Poker], all of a sudden I feel lethargic with no energy whatsoever. Hopefully it's what I call the "Brunson Blues." When I don't have something to gamble on, I start feeling bad. It's hard to call yourself a degenerate gambler, but I guess that's what I am. I've had 57 years of almost non stop gambling, and I need that adrenaline rush.[18]

He's not alone. Two columnists in one 2007 issue of *Card Player* magazine each referred to the majority of poker players as being addicted to the action, and thus more manipulable at the tables. "At their core, most poker players are action junkies, and they will sit in any poker game that fits their bankroll (and many that don't)," wrote poker player and writer Matt Matros.[19] A few pages earlier in the same issue, Todd Brunson, Doyle Brunson's son and a successful high-stakes player in his own right, made a similar observation in his column called "The Big Game": "Most poker players are degenerate action addicts, and although I've always denied this of myself, a little of this disease may live deep inside me."[20]

Stu "The Kid" Ungar may have been the greatest poker player of all time. A three-time World Series of Poker main event winner, including his dramatic comeback in 1997, Ungar was also a world-class gin rummy player. The wiry, brash New Yorker was obviously gifted. He was also a stone-cold gambling and drug addict. Ungar snorted so much cocaine that his nostrils apparently collapsed.[21] Though Ungar won hundreds of thousands of dollars at poker, he lost it all either on drugs, betting on sports, or horse races. After he died at age forty-five in a seedy Las Vegas motel room in 1998, an autopsy found the death to be accidental but drug-related. A mixture of cocaine, methadone, and Percodan found in his blood-stream most likely led to a heart condition that killed him, the Clark County coroner found.[22]

Ungar may be the most dramatic example of poker playing brilliance matched with addictive self-destruction. But his antics away from the poker table were never glorified like those of the top poker stars of the current generation. Top poker websites routinely run stories on the lavish homes of some pros and on their partying adventures at Las Vegas Strip nightclubs. And they spotlight the outlandish prop bets made by some of the players with headlines such as: "Ivey and Dwan's Vegetarian Bet Highlights High Stakes Poker: $1 Million Bet Booked on Ivey's Ability to Stay Away from Red Meat."[23] (Three weeks into the yearlong bet, Tom Dwan allowed Phil Ivey, generally considered to be the top poker player in the world as of 2010, to back out of the bet for $150,000.)

The only thing these prop bets have to do with poker is that they're ways for players to exercise their gambling jones and to show-case their complete disregard for money, an ability many poker play-ers believe is essential to be able to survive at the highest levels.

• • •

This lifestyle is aided by a poker tournament circuit that's also conducive to addictive gambling behaviors. In the poker trade media, it's rare to find stories attacking the pro tournament scene as fundamentally corrupt and driven by greed. Yet that's what poker author and current industry spokesman Nolan Dalla concluded in a 2003 story on the website PokerPages.com.[24] Dalla, the media director for the World Series of Poker, described a tournament circuit rife with top-name players who were actually constantly broke. They would borrow from other players or financial backers to stay in action and then often never pay them back, even when they won large amounts.

He also described instances where some players would intentionally oversell pieces of themselves, meaning percentage-stakes of their entries—so that, like in the Broadway show *The Producers*, after the players sold more than 100 percent of themselves, they could simply skim the profit off the top and then intentionally bust out of the tournament before making any money. And none of these groups could match offensiveness of the "railbirds," Dalla wrote, the aggressive group of player/spectators who line the rails of many tournaments. They're too poor to buy their way into tournaments but not too shameless to attach themselves to newly minted winners "like barnacles stuck to the side of a ship," to beg for handouts.

"What shocked me wasn't the ceaseless chicanery or the sullen faces of many on the tournament circuit so much as the degrees of *depravity* which currently exist in tournament poker," Dalla wrote.

"Sadly, tournament poker is filled with dishonest, dishonorable people. This is not to say that all tournament players are dishonest. Many tournament pros are decent people with loads of integrity . . . (Yet) the perpetual state of indebtedness has blurred the lines between right and wrong and created selfish incentives to default on commitments."

• • •

It would be difficult to lump in some of today's top professionals with Dalla's lot of reprobates. A couple immediately come to mind, like Erik Seidel, who holds eight World Series of Poker bracelets. A native New Yorker with a studious air, Seidel, fifty-one, dropped out of Brooklyn College to become a professional backgammon player. He drifted toward poker but took a hiatus from the wear and tear of professional gambling in 1985 to become a stockbroker, and held on through the stock market crash two years later before returning to poker. He's become one of the most consistent top tournament players—and by all accounts, manages his money successfully and lives a quiet family life in Las Vegas outside the poker room.

And then there's Chris "Jesus" Ferguson, probably known to more folks outside the poker universe than Seidel, with his distinctive Western duds, black cowboy hat, and long hair. Like Seidel, Ferguson, a Californian with a doctorate in computer science, concentrates on tournaments as opposed to cash games and takes a thoughtful and serious approach to the game. The winner of the 2000 World Series main event also likewise appears to maintain a full life outside of poker.

That said, both Seidel and Ferguson have a real advantage in being able to maintain their tournament bankrolls. They're both members of Team Full Tilt, the popular online poker site. Though Full Tilt's sponsorship policies with individual players aren't publicly known—a spokeswoman declined comment, saying the company was private—it is widely believed in the poker community that the tournament buy-ins for the fourteen players lucky enough to be team members are paid for by the site, and that they own a small-percentage stake in the company. That's a measure of financial security that so many pokers players, including those who claim and aspire to be real professionals, don't have.

•   •   •

Watch the World Series of Poker or the World Poker Tour on TV, and it's inevitable that the announcers describe many of the players as "poker pros." This, despite the fact that many of these players who reach the final table are unknowns and are never heard from again after that one tournament. That these players are described as professionals aids the notion—promoted by many in the industry—that becoming a poker pro is a relative breeze, as well as a sound career choice for large numbers of players. But even poker insiders concede this notion is bogus.

"There are a lot of gray areas in these definitions," said Justin Marchand, chief media officer for Card Player Media, in an interview at their offices in Las Vegas. He estimated that there were about 250 "hard core" poker tournament professionals—referring to live and not online tournament pros—who are able to buy into tournaments with their own money or are fully sponsored by an online site such as Full Tilt or PokerStars.com. There are roughly another one thousand in Las Vegas, he said, who can support themselves by winning at cash games at the prominent poker rooms on the Las Vegas Strip. There are many additional serious amateurs, he notes, but it is highly difficult to actually become a consistently winning poker professional, he said, especially without some sort of sponsorship deal.

Marchand, who has also been associate publisher of *Card Player* magazine for the last half-decade, said his advice to readers usually is to treat poker as a hobby, as opposed to a main source of income. Many of the most successful players he knows—and definitely the most well-rounded—have other full-time jobs and at least a semblance of a life outside the tables.

Marchand said he didn't know many players who had ruined themselves through poker, but he does know of many, including top-name players, who have lost most or all of what they made through poker by engaging in other forms of casino gambling like sports betting or blackjack. To be successful, he said, players need to be leak-free. "There are a lot of players who don't have systems in place to help keep them out of trouble," he said. *Card Player* runs stories about prop bets, he said, because they show a high-living side of poker that readers want to see. It's sort of like how some movie fans get a kick out of watching Access Hollywood or reading *People* magazine to see actor-celebrities engage in eccentric behavior. He noted that prop bet stories on his website get more page hits than average. "It's become a voyeuristic part of the poker scene," he said.

He acknowledged that some in the industry might be encouraging the false message that becoming a poker pro is easy and entails little risk. But responsibility also lies with players, he said, for being able to figure out that mathematically, "it's a tough proposition."

Professional poker player, author, and broadcast commentator Phil Gordon backs up many of Marchand's points. In a *New York Times* Q&A article, Gordon wrote he was able to beat the game because he managed his bankroll effectively, had no addictive leaks such as other gambling games, and viewed each poker hand as a business decision. "I'm not a 'gambler' by nature—I consider myself a 'strategic investor,'" he wrote. "In fact, what we do at the poker table isn't very different than what investment professionals do—we just get our results every two minutes instead of every few months or years."[25]

But most of his fellow poker pros approached their careers differently and as such were in far worse financial shape, Gordon wrote. He estimated that about 50 percent of the name pros seen regularly on television actually had a negative net worth. "Frightening, I know," he wrote. When asked what percentage of pro poker players were also compulsive gamblers, he responded this way:

> Ninety percent of the 'professional players' I know have some serious "leaks" that affect their ability to hold on to their money. Whether it's playing too big for their bankroll or betting on sports or casino games, these leaks have a way of keeping many of them completely broke no matter how much they win on the tourna-

ment circuit. One of the "requirements" to be a great player is being able to divorce yourself from money and its value. Making good decisions at the poker table means that you must have the ability to "put a Ferrari" in the pot if it's right to do so. That lack of respect for the buying power of money leads to financial problems for many of the best players in the world.

Others in the poker industry choose to downplay the risks. In a 2006 *Las Vegas Review-Journal* story, Howard Lederer, the successful poker tournament player who co-founded the Full Tilt online poker website, "maintained it would [be] hard to become a compulsive poker player 'based on the skill element. It is a skill-based game.'"[26]

In fact, it's an issue that judges around the country have weighed in recent years as they decide whether to legalize the game in poker clubs and private home games played for money. In many states, games that are viewed as more based on chance than skill are considered "gambling" and therefore illegal. But with poker's rise, legal challenges to this notion have arisen after police arrested people accused of running for-profit home games. In short, there has been no consensus. In South Carolina, a municipal judge found "overwhelming" evidence that poker was a game of skill.[27] A couple of years earlier, a three-judge panel with the North Carolina Court of Appeals found the opposite—that luck held sway enough of the time for poker legally to be considered a game of chance.

"All witnesses appeared to agree that in a single hand, chance may predominate over skill, but that over a long game, the most skilled players would likely amass the most chips," the panel found. Yet, although skills "such as knowledge of human psychology, bluffing, and the ability to calculate and analyze odds make it more likely for skilled players to defeat novices, novices may yet prevail with a simple run of luck. No amount of skill can change a deuce into an ace. Thus, the instrumentality for victory is not entirely in the player's hand."[28]

•　　•　　•

Tell that to T. J. Cloutier and he'd likely laugh in agreement. Cloutier, a burly Texan who's played tight end in the Canadian Football League and worked as an oil field laborer, has won almost $10 million in poker tournament scores in a storied career. But he knows well how luck can trump skill on any given hand. In the 2000 World Series main event, it came down to Cloutier and Chris Ferguson in a heads-up duel for the bracelet. After two hours of one on one play, Ferguson held a razor-thin lead over Cloutier, when he peeked down at his hand and found an ace of diamonds and a queen of clubs—a very strong hand with just two players. He raised, Ferguson raised back and Cloutier went all-in. After much deliberation, Ferguson called, with an ace of spades and a nine of clubs. Though he was disastrously far behind in the hand, Ferguson caught a miracle nine on the river, or the last card dealt, and won the championship. That was one example of skill getting beat by luck, as Ferguson himself immediately conceded.

Cloutier also plays craps. His yen for the game is well-known in the poker community, many of whom have seen him at casino craps tables betting black $100 chips. (I once saw Cloutier at a craps table in Caesars Palace in Las Vegas. Frequently a highly social game with lots of participants lined around the rectangular table clapping and urging one another on, he stood alone as he threw the dice.)

During an interview with a British poker website, he insisted that he hasn't lost the amount of money some people might think. He also said he likes to play craps and that "I really gamble with it sometimes." Further, he acknowledged that he uses the game as a way to get his gambling "fix."

"I regret that I'm so into it," Cloutier said. "But there's a fix for everyone in these Vegas casinos. People get into blackjack or high-stakes slots. When I want to get away, I get away with the craps."[29]

For whatever reason—and it's difficult not to make an educated guess that his craps-playing played a role—Cloutier was apparently sufficiently cash poor that in early 2010, he pawned two of his doz-

summer reading

DID YOU KNOW?

...it's for adults, too!

- Summer Reading is for **all ages**
- **Any reading counts** – books you read, or that you read to someone else
- **All reading counts** –books for children, teens, or adults; magazines; newspapers; e-books & audiobooks...if you read it, it counts
- There are also **<u>activities</u>** you can do to earn points
- Earn a **free tote bag** and a coupon for a **free book** and be entered into the **Grand Prize drawings**
- See staff for more info or with any questions, and register at:

www.saclibrary.org/summerreading

 SACRAMENTO PUBLIC LIBRARY
www.saclibrary.org

June 1 – August 15, 2018

ens of championship poker bracelets to a pawnshop in Plano, Texas. When called by an online poker show producer about the matter, Cloutier said he didn't want to talk about it, other than to say he pawned the items because he was "short," or low on money.[30]

Phil Laak seems about as different from Cloutier as two poker pros could be. Cloutier is a friendly but reserved Texan; Laak, raised in Massachusetts, likes pulling attention-getting stunts. But like Cloutier, Laak has been forthright about how his gambling has affected him for the worse.

Laak is known as an eccentric in a poker community full of them. Over the years he's tried to build on the image. In 2008, a professional makeup artist helped disguise him as an elderly poker player for the World Series main event. Two years later, he established a new Guinness World Record for the longest continuous poker session in history. He played for 115 hours straight in a $10-$20 no-limit Hold'em cash game at the Bellagio poker room in Las Vegas. (He was allowed five-minute breaks every hour.)

In a 2007 newspaper interview, Laak, the boyfriend of poker-playing actress Jennifer Tilly, talked about how in his early poker years he was literally "sick" for the game. Once, when he was away from gambling for a couple of days, he said he got physically ill, like an alcoholic forced to stop drinking.[31]

"I do believe there's a certain part of you that does have to go hard-core for the game," he said. "There were six months in my life I was totally sick for the game. I couldn't get enough. I once went on a ski trip and I started having withdrawals, shakes, because I had not made a bet with anybody over anything for two-and-a-half days. I came back [to Las Vegas], and I joined the game and I ended up playing poker for three days straight."

CHAPTER 5

The Online Fix

At first, the shy, sandal-wearing computer whiz named Anurag Dik-shit found only moderate career success in the United States. He hailed from a small industrial town in eastern India called Sindri and graduated from the prestigious Indian Institute of Technology in New Delhi before moving to the States in the mid-1990s. Initially he worked as a systems analyst for a group called Websci, and later as a consultant for AT&T.[1]

But Dikshit (pronounced "Dixit") anticipated the dot-com boom with world-class timing—ultimately cashing in to a degree he must have thought unimaginable. His fortunes changed when he agreed to work with Ruth Parasol, the sex chat line and Internet pornography mini-mogul.[2] Parasol had sold her porn business and, sensing an untapped market in Internet gambling, decided to try to exploit it in 1997 with the online Starluck Casino. To make her new venture really take hold, she needed an imaginative, first-rate software writer to develop new proprietary codes for online gambling programs. After meeting through a friend of a friend, Dikshit, then twenty-five, agreed to write programs for online roulette and blackjack for Parasol's company, PartyGaming.

Noting the fast-growing success of a rival online site, Dikshit and Parasol switched their focus to online poker. That set the stage for the launch of PartyPoker in 2001, an offshoot of PartyGaming. Though they weren't the first to enter the online poker market, they quickly became the biggest—and in the process, incredibly rich. By the time PartyGaming went public on the London Stock Exchange in June 2005, the company was valued at the equivalent of more than $8 billion.[3] The following year, Dikshit was ranked by Forbes as the 207th richest person in the world, with a net worth of $3.3 billion.[4]

A big chunk of PartyGaming's profits came from American online gamblers. Specifically, from poker players who relished finding a way to play their favorite game with global competitors and from the comfort of their homes. But that changed quickly for PartyPoker, which stopped accepting American gamblers after Congress passed the Unlawful Internet Gambling Enforcement Act of 2006 (UIGEA). The measure made it illegal for funds to be transferred from financial institutions to online gambling sites. The new law made it tougher, and legally risky, for Americans to deposit money on these sites.

Still, Dikshit felt compelled to further settle things with the U.S. Justice Department—whose agents by then had arrested other international Internet gambling tycoons for violating the Federal Wire Act. (Unlike some federal judges who have studied the issue, the Justice Department has maintained that the Wire Act makes all online gambling illegal.) In 2008, he pleaded guilty and agreed to pay a $300 million fine for violating the act. Neither Parasol's nor PartyGaming's other stunned principals followed suit. "I came to believe it was in fact illegal under U.S. law," Dikshit told a U.S. District Court judge at a hearing in New York, referring to PartyGaming's activity. "I have taken full responsibility for my actions."[5]

Dikshit, who lives in Gibraltar, sold his last remaining shares of PartyGaming stock in January 2010. All told, he made $1.1 billion from his stock sales, about $800 million of which was headed for his philanthropy, the Kusuma Foundation.

Over the years, Dikshit has avoided the press. A London-based spokesman for the online mogul named Shimon Cohen said by e-mail this was still the case. When asked whether Dikshit had ever expressed concerns about playing a key role in expanding the availability of a highly addictive type of gambling, Cohen declined to answer. He instead noted that, "During the time Anurag was involved with this company, he was supportive of the company's Responsibility Programme." The problem gambling program offered by PartyGaming—whose poker site is poised to make a big comeback in America should ongoing efforts to scrap the 1996 UIGEA law be successful—includes allowing players to self-limit how much money they can deposit into the site and how much time they spend playing, and to exclude themselves from the site for "cooling off periods" of up to six months or longer if they feel they've been playing too much.[6]

"We are committed to providing a secure and responsible online gaming environment," PartyGaming's website maintains. "Our position on responsible gaming is clear: we want everyone who plays at one of our online sites to be there for the right reason—to have fun."

Online wagering, the industry Dikshit helped build, has snowballed into the biggest gambling trend worldwide. Gamblers first became connected to one another by means of a virtual casino in 1995. Since then, more than two thousand Internet gambling sites have opened.[7] Yet what's caused its popularity to spike—primarily its convenience and speedy pace compared with live gambling games in casinos—are the same dynamics that have made online gambling especially addictive, studies and addiction experts confirm. These troubles could escalate if the persistent congressional efforts to overturn the UIGEA law are successful.

Traversing through cyberspace, whether it involves shopping for sunglasses or playing hand after hand of Texas Hold'em, is by and large a solitary endeavor. Sure, online gamblers are connected to one another and often can "chat" through small written posts. But each gambler is almost always sitting alone while playing, unlike at a casino. Add that to the ability of online gamblers to play significantly faster than they're able to at casinos, and the reasons for the higher rates of addiction are clear.

The young, especially college students and recent grads, are especially at risk of developing Internet gambling problems, studies show. They are not only wired to a much greater degree than their parents, they're also more likely to gamble.

The National Gambling Impact Study Commission warned of these potential problems in its 1999 report, issued when the online industry was relatively tiny compared to its current state. "In addition to their accessibility, the high-speed instant gratification of Internet games and the high level of privacy they offer may exacerbate problem and pathological gambling," the report's authors concluded.[8] Since then the threat has been realized, according to prominent research studies conducted over the decade since the commission's report. They've detailed how pathological online gambling is connected to poor physical and mental health even more than other forms of gambling.

Betting on the Internet is a radically different type of gambling experience than "social gambling" like kitchen-table card games or office football pools, said Les Bernal, executive director of the group Stop Predatory Gambling, in a *New York Times* article. How so? "The speed of the game, the frequency of play (gambling operators allow users to play multiple games at once), the intensity of the high or buzz people get when they play, and the enormous amount of money people lose, all of which goes down twenty-four hours a day, seven days a week," Bernal wrote. "It is the equivalent of opening a Las Vegas casino in every house, apartment, and dorm room in America."[9]

Despite the 2006 UIGEA law, the phenomenon has boomed. Ten million Americans play poker online for money (as opposed to the free, not-for-money games most of the sites also host).[10] That's an exponentially higher number of players than in any other nation. The country that came the closest in the 2009 survey was the United Kingdom, with 1.9 million players. Germany and France were next on the list, with 1.6 million and 1.3 million players respectively. A different survey a year later estimated that American gamblers would bet $5.7 billion online by the end of 2010, down slightly from the $6 billion wagered in 2006. According to the same analysis, Americans comprised 17.2 percent of the worldwide online gambling market.[11]

Analysts predict that online gambling in the United States would explode if UIGEA is repealed. Bills on the table from Democratic U.S. representatives Barney Frank (Mass.) and Jim McDermott (Wash.)— as well as efforts from state lawmakers around the country—would effectively put the kibosh on the law if passed.

According to the British consulting group H2 Gambling Capital, if all forms of Internet gambling were fully legalized across the country except sports betting, which appears to be the least likely type of gambling to be sanctioned online, $67 billion would be generated for the U.S. economy over the first five years. This would generate $30 billion in new federal taxes and spur the creation of more than 125,000 jobs, the group predicted.[12]

According to online proponents, federal and state government coffers are missing out on an untapped tax base. Europe's example should be followed, they submit. Europe has become the biggest online gambling market in the world, accounting for 43 percent of total worldwide revenues. Britain led the way in 2005, and Italy has also been in the process of legalizing online gambling in stages. Some European countries have moved from a hostile stance regarding online gambling companies toward acceptance and legalization. France, like the United States, has jailed top online company officials. But more recently they've welcomed officials from the same companies into their country with open arms. From Denmark to Greece, European governments as of 2010 were uniformly trending toward accepting online gambling and deregulating the business by allowing private companies to compete with state-sponsored gambling sites.[13]

Some officials, noting the correlation between online gambling and high addiction rates, have claimed that legalization is wise because conscientious government controls can aid in protecting problem gamblers. But this has raised the same concerns that have taken hold in U.S. states—that reliance on gambling revenues, which partly come from addicted gamblers, is distorting the appropriate role of government and creating dependencies of more than one type.

It's not just gambling critics raising issues about Europe's growing reliance on taxes from online gambling. "I think the penny has dropped," Simon Holliday, an analyst with H2 Gambling Capital, told the *New York Times*. "They deregulate a little bit, like what happens and deregulate more. The governments get more addicted to the tax than the players to the games."[14]

Two main laws are at the heart of the current congressional debate over online gambling, UIGEA and another measure passed years before the Internet, or even personal computers, existed. The Wire Communications Act of 1961, also known as the Interstate Wire Act, outlawed the use of a "wire communication facility" for the transmission of interstate or international bets or wagers. It also made the use of such facilities to provide information on how to place bets on sporting events or contests illegal. The bill was put forth in part to try to prevent organized crime from gaining traction in the gambling industry.

The Justice Department has interpreted the Wire Act to mean that all online gambling is illegal, period. In addition to concerns about problem gamblers being forged in front of computer screens, federal officials have noted the potential for fraud, money laundering, and gambling among minors. These positions have remained consistent throughout the administrations of Presidents Bill Clinton, George W. Bush, and Barack Obama.

Deputy Assistant Attorney General Kevin Di Gregory, testifying before a House subcommittee in 1998, explained that states were likely to seek federal assistance when foreign-based, online casinos offered gambling to its citizens in violation of local law. "Assisting states through enforcement of the Wire Communications Act, therefore, is fully consistent with the department's law enforcement priorities," he said.[15]

Five years later, a different deputy assistant attorney general, John Malcolm, honed in on the risks to gamblers as he spoke to a Senate committee: "Unlike on-site gambling, on-line gambling is readily available to all at all hours, and it permits the user to gamble, in many cases, anonymously. This presents a greater danger for compulsive gambling and can cause severe financial consequences for an unsuccessful player," he said.[16]

Several online gambling site owners and operators have been detained or arrested in the last decade for violating the Wire Act. In 2000, Jay Cohen became the first person to be convicted of running an illegal offshore Internet sports gambling operation. Cohen, co-owner of World Sports Exchange, based in Antigua, was sentenced to twenty-one months in prison and was fined $5,000. Six years later, David Carruthers, the former chief executive of an online company called BetOnSports, and ten others were indicted on Wire Act violations. He was sentenced to thirty-three months in prison in 2010 after pleading guilty. BetOnSports, which was based in London, took in $1.25 billion in 2004. No less than 98 percent of the revenue came from bets by U.S.–based gamblers, according to court papers.

Online gambling proponents, especially poker website operators, have argued persistently that the Wire Act only applies to sports bets, and not to games like poker. Several federal judges have agreed with them. In a case involving the alleged violations of online casinos and lotteries, a U.S. District Court judge in 2001 found that the Wire Act did not apply. Several years later, the judge's ruling was upheld by a panel from the 5th U.S. Circuit Court of Appeals. The U.S. Supreme Court has never addressed whether Internet gambling other than sports betting is covered by the Wire Act.

As online gambling and especially Internet poker took off, Justice Department officials recognized the deficiencies of the Wire Act and urged Congress to try to clarify the law so that it was clear that all types of Internet gambling were illegal.

Online gambling opponents, who passed UIGEA in 2006, hoped the law would provide such a clarification. But the law has been controversial from the start. For starters, it slid through Congress in the most secretive manner possible, buried deep inside an unrelated piece of legislation about security at U.S. ports.

The measure was also decried because of its convoluted nature, and the claim that it relied on banks to act as law enforcement agents to make sure their customers weren't circumventing the law. Ultimately, it may have slowed Internet gambling in the United States, but it hasn't come close to stopping it.

The law, which didn't take full effect until June 1, 2010, on its face did not make it illegal for Americans to place bets online, or impossible. But make no mistake: players using the sites to buy into cash games or tournaments need to use credit or debit cards or some other type of online payment system so that the money reaches offshore Internet gambling sites. If using these payment systems isn't illegal in itself, players unquestionably are bumping right up against activity that is illegal—the transfer of funds from financial institutions to foreign-based online gambling sites. (Online horse race wagering, legal in certain states, was carved out as an exception to the restrictions.)

Because of online gambling's quasi-illegal status and renewed law enforcement warnings about the activity, the 2006 law pushed some nervous recreational gamblers away from online gambling. The law also caused several online poker and other gambling sites such as PartyPoker, bwin, and Sportingbet to stop accepting deposits from U.S. customers.

Historically, the government has primarily targeted sports betting website owners for prosecution, not poker site operators—and certainly not Internet poker players or their money. Experts generally have considered poker to be in a different legal category from online sports betting, in part because the Wire Act directly mentions only sports betting. Online poker advocates also believe that UIGEA doesn't apply to them because poker involves a transaction between gamblers, not a bet or wager between a gambler and the casino. And there's a further legal distinction, they argue, because poker is a game of skill and not chance (as discussed in the previous chapter).

The fact that individual bettors haven't been targeted for criminal violations has made it easier for millions of online gamblers to play, without caring who knows it. It's also caused many to believe that what they are doing is in keeping with the spirit of the law, even as they're regularly being forced to find new ways to deposit money into these sites.

Although no arrests of online gamblers have yet been made, the feds have begun applying new types of pressure—including for the first time hitting gamblers in their pocketbooks. In mid-2009, soon before the World Series of Poker was set to start in Las Vegas, federal prosecutors requested that several banks freeze $33 million in payments owed to about twenty-seven thousand poker players who had been playing at different poker sites, including the two that are far and away the most popular among American players, PokerStars and Full Tilt. The banks complied, raising the ire of thousands of gamblers whose checks bounced. Unlike PartyPoker, those two sites stuck around after the UIGEA law was passed, willing to brave the hostile American law enforcement climate in order to make millions of dollars in the small amounts of "rake" they take from every virtual poker pot.

Washington, D.C., attorney A. Jeff Ifrah, who has represented PokerStars and Full Tilt since 2007, told me that the twenty-seven thousand poker players whose money was frozen were made whole by the sites within a couple of weeks of the story becoming public. The sites did this even though they never got back the $33 million seized by the federal government. Moreover, even though it hasn't been noted in the press, Ifrah said that the initial seizure by Justice Department was followed by thirteen more, if smaller, seizures of poker players' cash.

Each of the seizures, he said, involved cases in which the companies that had been processing payouts on behalf of online poker sites were alleged to have lied to banks by claiming that the funds were not coming from gambling sites. That constitutes bank fraud, and the easily discoverable lies made the cases fairly easy to prosecute, he said.

According to Ifrah, the Justice Department is after the funds of Internet gamblers, not the gamblers themselves. In the case of the frozen $33 million, the funds were forfeited to the feds after the man who operated one of those payout processing companies, Account Services, pled guilty to using the wires to transmit bets and wagering information in interstate commerce in May of 2010. The victims, Ifrah said, are the players who have done nothing wrong.

"I've had calls from med school students, law students, work-at-home moms," said Ifrah. "They're upset because they rely on this money."

Ifrah said the Justice Department's concern about problem gambling among online players is clear. Agency officials raise the issue every time he and his poker website clients communicate with the department, he said. "The number one issue for them is underage gambling, and the number two issue is problem gambling," he said. He said that the sites he represents are cognizant of the issues and have taken steps to address them. Regarding problem gambling, "they have procedures in place to recognize that type of behavior, and they will turn off players" when appropriate to do so, he said, meaning barring them from the site. "I know they've turned off players."

Ifrah has visited the offshore headquarters of PokerStars in the Isle of Man, and Full Tilt in Dublin, Ireland. He said the companies have been diligent about monitoring the games on their sites, and had other advanced technological safeguards in place to make sure no underage players found their way into the games, that players weren't exhibiting addictive behaviors, and that no collusion or other forms of cheating were taking place.

Although those operating the poker sites believe what they're doing is completely legal, Ifrah noted there has been concern that the Justice Department could be targeting them next for arrest. "Of course they worry about that," he said. "It's a good question. Why haven't the feds done anything? It kind of stuns everybody."

In the past, government agents have nabbed Internet gambling operators during visits to the United States, including brief airline stop-overs. People close to one of the primary owners of Poker-Stars, an Israeli named Isai Scheinberg, have said he doesn't visit the United States for this reason. It's unclear exactly who owns Full Tilt. Ifrah said the company is privately held and doesn't divulge that information publicly. The two American professional poker players most directly affiliated with the site—and who have been rumored to have small ownership stakes—Howard Lederer and Chris Ferguson, live in Las Vegas, so presumably the FBI could track them down if they wanted. Repeated requests to talk to either of them through a Full Tilt spokeswoman went unanswered.

Another Vegas resident, Doyle Brunson, the "Godfather of Poker" who turned seventy-seven in 2010, is closely affiliated with the Costa Rica–based DoylesRoom.com poker site that he founded with co-investors in 2004. He has regularly promoted it since to U.S.–based players. Though he's said he doesn't own the site, he is a stockholder. Regardless, he hasn't backed away from his investment, which he believes is legal in the United States. "I don't have a problem with the Justice Department, and I hope they don't have a problem with me," he says. "At my age I really don't care if they are going to cast the gauntlet."[17]

Online gambling proponents, spurred by a group headed by former New York Republican senator Alfonse D'Amato called the Poker Players Alliance, made some headway in 2010 in scrapping the UIGEA law. In July, Congressman Frank's bill, which would direct the Treasury Department to regulate online gambling sites, passed out of the House Financial Services Committee by a vote of forty-one to twenty-two. It was the biggest victory to date for online gambling supporters.

Looking forward, legal analysts say it's unlikely that Congress will pass Frank's bill any time soon, or its companion legislation being pushed by Representative McDermott, which would allow Internet gambling to be taxed. The federal budget crunch has helped prod the bills' limited success so far. But there is enough of a coalition against the measures—including religious conservatives and liberal Democrats concerned about the social impacts of the bill, and law enforcement advocates in agreement with the Justice Department's constant warnings—that their long-term prognosis appears gloomy.

A more likely scenario for the legalization of online gambling may lie with the states, these analysts say—a trend that should come as no surprise. As we've seen, state lawmakers typically are not reluctant to support legalized gambling as a way to avoid making tough choices over how to raise revenues and balance budgets.

A number of states have been weighing whether to try to legalize online gambling within their own borders. As of mid-2010, legislators in New Jersey, Florida, and California were proposing to legalize various forms of Internet gambling. Nevada lawmakers also have weighed the issue. Proponents believe that states would be able to take advantage of a provision in the 2006 UIGEA law that could permit the activity as long as it does not cross state lines.

If one of these bills passes, it's likely to prompt "a new wave of similar movements in other states, particularly those which already have land-based gambling," notes poker writer and World Series of Poker spokesman Nolan Dalla. The outcome of several states allowing intrastate Internet gambling could be that pacts of these states then could allow for interstate online poker. Dalla notes that a similar thing happened with the legalization of state lotteries. "[L]egalized online poker could reach millions of poker players, one state at a time, until a broad coalition of businesses and organizations, both public and private, takes shape."[18]

To be sure, online poker operators are waiting to pounce if and when the time comes that it's fully legalized. None are planning more diligently than PartyGaming. In 2009, the company purchased the World Poker Tour (WPT), the popular series of televised high-profile live tournaments. More recently, the business signed a new contract with its well-regarded spokesman, Mike Sexton, and two other known poker commentators. Sexton has served both as the lead commentator on WPT broadcasts, as well as PartyPoker's most visible promoter before the company left the U.S. market. "It's all part of a plan to reclaim what was lost with UIGEA. When Party led the exodus from the U.S. market, there was speculation that once the industry became regulated, such cooperation and adherence would be remembered by the U.S. government," a 2010 ESPN.com story concluded.[19]

As politicians in Congress and the states weigh what to do about online gambling's future, they might want to take heed of a couple of 2010 surveys on the topic. In August, *The Week* magazine's website asked its readers whether Congress should legalize online gambling in order to bolster tax revenues. Fifty-two percent of the readers said no, to only 31 percent who answered yes.[20] (The rest were split about evenly between answering "perhaps" and "none of the above.") Several months earlier, in a national poll conducted by Fairleigh Dickinson University's survey research group, just over one thousand people were questioned about their thoughts on different gambling-related topics. Respondents made it even more clear they did not want to see more online gambling. Two-thirds of those polled said no when asked if they wanted the law changed to allow people to place bets over the Internet.[21] According to these two surveys, it seems clear that fully legalizing and regulating online gambling is an unpopular idea.

There's at least one understandable reason for this. Gamblers and non-gamblers alike seem to know instinctively what the bulk of the research concludes: gambling over the Internet is even more addictive than other forms of gambling; there's a direct correlation between the activity and decreased physical and mental health; and the young are especially at risk.

In a study of more than 1,350 college students on three different university campuses, researchers from the University of Connecticut (UConn) found that one in four had gambled on the Internet at least once—"substantially higher than that noted in samples of adults," as much as four times higher, the researchers found.[22] Thirteen percent of the sample said they gambled online a lot, anywhere from more than ten times in their lives, to every day. But here's the more shocking statistic: the study, released in 2007, found that one-third of those students who had ever gambled online could be classified as "probable pathological gamblers." To put it another way, one in three college students who tried it were found to be gambling addicts. "The present study, similarly to others, found that Internet gambling is closely related to pathological gambling behaviors," the researchers concluded. They noted that they couldn't say with certainty whether the students' online gambling caused the problematic behavior, whether those who already gambled problematically were prone to gamble on the Internet—or whether both trends were at least partially true, as common sense would dictate is likely the case.

The UConn researchers also found that Internet gambling was

a "statistically significant predictor" of poor mental health. "These data suggest that Internet gambling is an especially troublesome activity, and prevention, early intervention, and treatment efforts may need to be targeted toward college students who wager on the Internet," the researchers found. But this may prove to be difficult, they noted, as students are unlikely to concede they've got a problem—and almost no college campuses offer services specifically for problem gamblers.

A larger survey conducted in Sweden also showed troubling numbers. Of 16,500 Swedish adults polled in 2006 about their online playing habits, researchers concluded that 27 percent of those who played poker online were problem gamblers.[23] The one-year survey by the Swedish National Institute of Public Health, mirroring other studies, found that Internet gamblers were primarily young and male. Of the roughly 140,000 adults who played online poker on a monthly basis during 2006, men outnumbered women by a ratio of ten to one, and the average age of the players was twenty-five.

"[T]he results are that the game of poker online is indeed creating more problem gamblers than other gaming outlets," concluded the Washington, D.C.–based National Council on Problem Gambling in a news release about the Swedish study.[24] The council has argued that if online gambling is legalized, proper regulation is key to trying to prevent problem gambling. That means creating the ability of both players and online operators to set limits on time played and money deposited to the sites, as well as the power of players to self-exclude themselves from sites should they feel it necessary. Keith Whyte, the council's executive director, testified before Congress on Representative Frank's bill that online problem gambling programs could be improved by using player data the sites collect to develop profiles of online wagering behavior. That information, he said, could be used as an important prevention tool by helping to build programs to show what constitutes a normal amount of online play as opposed to "abnormal usage."[25]

• • •

Tales of such abnormal attachments to online gambling and the destruction it wrought increasingly came to light in the early 2000s. As online gambling exploded, stories seeped in the poker world about twenty-two-year-olds who regularly played more than a dozen Internet poker games simultaneously and won hundreds of thousands of dollars through their virtual poker prowess. That meant others were losing just as fast. Legions of these new online fanatics, including many college students, were hooked almost instantly and couldn't stop losing.

Greg Hogan Jr. became the most famous example of someone turned upside down by the trend. When he entered Lehigh University, Hogan's prospects seemed strong. The son of a minister, he was highly talented pianist and cellist who had appeared twice in Carnegie Hall. A popular student, Hogan became his sophomore class president.

He also caught the poker bug soon after he matriculated, which almost immediately turned into a raging addiction to online poker. By the end of his spree, in late 2005, he was borrowing money from whomever he could and playing fourteen-hour sessions in his fraternity's lounge or the school library. "As soon as I lost, I had to get more money in my account immediately," he told the *New York Times*. "My whole body was shaking as I waited for the program to load, I wanted to play so badly."[26]

Heading off to see a movie with friends one day, Hogan, nineteen, asked a friend to find a bank so he could cash a check. He then robbed the Allentown, Pennsylvania, bank branch by passing a teller a note falsely claiming he had a gun. He walked out with $2,871, but was arrested that evening as he arrived at university orchestra practice. Hogan served a twenty-two-month sentence. He's avoided the press since his release from Huntingdon State Prison in mid-2008. But his father, Greg Hogan Sr., has spoken out, and said that his son has told him that he's remained bet-free since before he started serving his sentence and has been regularly attending Gamblers Anonymous meetings since.[27]

Testifying before Congress against Frank's bill to fully legalize and regulate online gambling, Hogan Sr., a Baptist preacher from a small Ohio city outside Akron, said his son's Internet gambling addiction had also victimized him and his wife and three other children, each of whom had suffered depression and sleep disturbances.[28] To best explain his thoughts about what Congress was considering, he turned to his pastoral teachings.

"Saint Paul challenges us in his epistle to the Romans, 'And why not say, Let us do evil that good may come?' Every argument for the legalization or expansion of gambling from a governmental official, to me, has a common thread: 'We can do so much good with the money we get from gambling,'" Hogan testified. "Has our government which was created to protect the common good become just as addicted to gambling as my son was when he walked into that bank?"

Michael Sandberg also became something of a media poster boy for the online poker surge, with appearances in the *New York Times*, HBO's *Real Sports with Bryant Gumbel,* and *The Daily Show* with Jon Stewart. His story has a happier ending than Hogan's, but it's still a cautionary tale of sorts.

As a politics major at Princeton, Sandberg was an online poker phenom. From his room on the top floor of his dorm, the Alexandria, Virginia, native many days would alternate between studying and playing up to ten hours a day on PartyPoker. From September 2004 through the following March, he earned $90,000 through the online games and another $30,000 during trips to Atlantic City. At the time, he told a reporter that although graduation was rapidly approaching, he had no plans for graduate school or even a traditional job. Poker was his career choice, he said. "I want to get to the point where I'm the best in the world and play against those guys on TV," he said.[29]

After graduation, he moved to Florida with his girlfriend. He continued to play online and continued to make money, about $10,000 per month, while working for his father's photography business, Sandberg told me in a telephone interview. After several months, the couple bought a house. The newfound responsibility changed him, he said, and caused him to think differently about what kind of future he wanted. "I don't know if I'd say I got tired of [poker]," he said. "I knew I wanted to do something more significant with my life." He applied to Capital University Law School in Columbus, Ohio, and got in. He said his poker diminished out of his desire to do as well as possible in school, and not just be willing to settle for the Bs he got at Princeton. He graduated in 2009, and when I spoke with him, he was serving as a judicial law clerk in Wicomico County, Maryland. He lives with his wife and a young child and aspires to become an environmental policy lawyer in Washington, D.C. He still plays a bit online, he said, but no more than four hours per week.

Sandberg said he's never thought of himself as a problem gambler. He was able to keep his emotions in check, and thought of his poker playing like it was a job or a trade. He was able to compartmentalize his poker. But his constant playing did affect him for the worse in college in some ways, he said. He didn't take his studies as seriously as he should have. And the sedentary lifestyle caused him to balloon to 265 pounds. He said he's now back down to 200. He noted that he's played with many others who clearly did have problems controlling themselves at the tables, be they real or in cyberspace. One guy in his group of college friends lost every single time they went to Atlantic City, he said. There were others, skilled or not, who went "on tilt," or became temporarily enraged, which caused them to try to get their money back at all costs when losing. "Honestly, I preyed on those people. I tried to get in pots with them," he said.

Sandberg said he believed that if he had chosen to become a

pro poker player and moved to Las Vegas, he could have one or two million in the bank by now. He might be right. Or he might have followed the paths of other would-be pros who live with little stability and wild financial swings, and sometimes hit the wall and go broke. Regardless, he said he believes he's on the right path. Had he tried the professional gambling route, "I doubt that my life would feel as fulfilling as it does right now," he said.

Representatives of the online poker industry have rebuffed the notion that Internet gambling is inherently addictive. Addressing the House Judiciary Committee on behalf of the Poker Players Alliance, which at the time claimed 800,000 American members, Annie Duke, a well-known tournament player, belittled the idea that online gambling posed serious risks of addiction. She cited a British 2007 gambling prevalence study that showed that the overall incidence of problem gambling in the United Kingdom had remained the same since the government studied the issue in 1999, before Internet gambling exploded. She also significantly underrepresented the number of problem and pathological gamblers in the United States. She claimed that of those adults who gambled in the United States, less than 1 percent were problem gamblers.[30]

In fact, of the U.S. adult population generally—and not of just those who gamble—about 1 percent of the population, or two million people, are widely thought to be pathological gamblers in any given year, according to the most comprehensive studies on the topic. An additional 2 to 3 percent of adults, equaling four to six million people, are thought to be problem gamblers, according to the National Council on Problem Gambling. That comes to six to eight million Americans who are experiencing moderate to severe gambling problems. Even the American Gaming Association, the trade group for the commercial casino industry, largely concedes these prevalence rates. The only difference is that the AGA believes that 2 percent of

Americans are problem gamblers, instead of the 2 to 3 percent figure more widely believed to be accurate.

Duke went on to compare problem gambling to excessive chocolate eating and water drinking. "Frankly, if the government is going to ban every activity that can lead to harmful compulsion, the government is going to have to ban nearly every activity," she testified. "Shopping, day trading, sex, chocolate, even drinking water—these and myriad other activities, most of which are a part of everyday life, have been linked to harmful compulsions. Are we going to move inexorably toward a world where we prohibit online shopping because some people compulsively spend themselves into bankruptcy?"[31]

Duke is the sister of Howard Lederer. Like Lederer, Duke also has had a business relationship with an online poker site that stands to benefit considerably should online poker be fully legalized. For several years through the end of 2010, she was connected to UB.com (more commonly known as UltimateBet), where she was listed as a member of Team UB along with about a dozen other players.[32]

In response to questions to a spokeswoman with the Poker Players Alliance about online problem gambling, including questions about Duke's testimony, the group offered a concise reply: "PPA's overarching belief . . . is that the best way to help curb addiction and protect problem gamblers is through federal licensing and regulation."

Top gambling researchers believe there are two main types of gambling addicts. "Escape" gamblers mostly stick to slot machines and lottery or scratch tickets, and "action" gamblers generally like to bet on sports, horse races, card and dice games, and the like. Most of the games that offer a skill component, such as poker, including online poker, are action games. In action games, as players bet, and as they anticipate making the bet, their neurological response has been likened to that of cocaine addicts. The heart races and the blood rushes.

One of the main risks of online gambling from an addiction standpoint is its faster pace and the ability to play several games at once, called "multi-tabling." This increases the action component exponentially beyond that of a live casino poker game. It takes the concept of action, the gambling rush, to a different level.

Online poker sites recognize this. Full Tilt, in fact, built a whole new game around the concept of speed called Rush Poker. The site's promotion page hypes it as "[T]he World's Fastest Poker Game!" A television ad featuring Full Tilt spokesman Phil Ivey notes its appeal: "It's more hands, more action. Why wouldn't you want to play Rush Poker?"

In Rush Poker, a relatively new phenomenon as of mid-2010, players don't have to wait for the completion of a hand to move on to the next one. As soon as they win the pot or fold their hand, they automatically move to a new hand, usually with new competitors. Moreover, if they're planning on folding, they are encouraged to do so before the action gets to them. At that point, the site immediately places them with other players from the same pool and deals them a new hand—a process usually lasting no more than a second or two.

It doesn't have the feel of a normal online game, let alone a poker game in an actual brick-and-mortar casino. This is mainly because the pace is incessant. Full Tilt's Rush Poker promotion page has a short introductory video by site spokesman Phil Gordon, in which he brags about players being dealt "hundreds and hundreds of hands per hour. It's amazing. It's like multi-tabling at a single table."[33] By contrast, the supervisors at poker rooms in two Las Vegas casinos estimated to me that in their Texas Hold'em games, players are typically dealt anywhere from twenty to thirty-six hands per hour.

It's unclear whether the game ultimately will catch on. It's also too soon to tell whether it will be blamed for setting a new standard of online gambling addictiveness. According to Gordon, one thing is clear: "Rush Poker is the coolest thing to happen to poker in a really long time."

CHAPTER 6

Evolving Science, Questionable Research

Since the 1920s, the tobacco industry has used public relations to help spin the sophisticated pleasures of cigarette smoking. Even as concerns began to mount over tobacco's health risks during the next couple decades, PR and marketing efforts helped turn smoking into an integral part of many Americans' social lives—"an indicator of social and cultural power, autonomy and attractiveness," according to the historian Allan M. Brandt.[1]

As data steadily accrued that confirmed cigarettes were cancer-causing and highly addictive, tobacco's PR campaign fundamentally changed in the early 1950s. Instead of trying to create new users by touting the appeal of cigarettes, the industry was in a defensive crouch, fending off attacks about the links between use of its products and rising rates of lung cancer. After retaining public relations giant Hill & Knowlton, executives from several tobacco firms approved an effort to fund their own studies.

They concluded they needed research that resulted in tobacco's exoneration. Tobacco's PR advisors suggested that neither direct attacks on scientists nor general assurances of safety would work. Both were shortsighted tactics, wrote Brandt in *The Cigarette Century: The Rise, Fall, and Deadly Persistence of the Product That Defined America*. Instead, they found that "seizing control of the science of tobacco and health would be as important as seizing control of the media. It would be critical to identify scientists who expressed skepticism about the link between cigarettes and cancer, those critical of statistical methods, and especially those who had offered alternative hypotheses for the cause of cancer."[2]

Thus began Big Tobacco's much-reviled history of underwriting its own research, often through the use of benign-sounding organizations, to make nicotine appear to be nonaddictive and cigarettes safe.

When gambling industry executives decided to fund their own research, they understood the need to do things differently. Clearly, they had watched with interest as the top tobacco company officials, known as the "Seven Dwarfs," stood in a row and raised their right hands before a congressional committee in 1994, each to proclaim under oath that nicotine wasn't addictive.

From the founding two years later of the National Center for Responsible Gaming (NCRG)—the charity group affiliated with the American Gaming Association (AGA)—the groups' leaders recognized denying the existence of problem gambling was no longer a viable option. Big Gambling had to concede that its customers could become addicted gamblers, just like some scotch drinkers, cocaine users, and smokers become addicted.

"Our industry cannot afford to make the mistake made by the tobacco industry years ago," AGA President and CEO Frank Fahrenkopf Jr. said in a Las Vegas speech to industry honchos soon after NCRG was formed in 1996. "When the assault against tobacco began, at their own peril, the industry failed to admit that there were problems and stalled in their commitment to acting responsible to deal with them. Today they are paying a heavy, heavy price, which, in addition to billions of dollars, could include the indictment for perjury of a few CEOs."[3]

In the same speech, Fahrenkopf noted that the media had been telling hundreds of stories about the gambling industry—and that problem gambling was mentioned "almost without exception." Such stories, often with anecdotes about "the ruination of innocent people," could sway a public that generally had supported legalized gambling, he said. "The growth of our industry is certainly endangered by the issue and, it is not hyperbole to say that the industry's very existence is at stake. We must respond appropriately and—importantly—proactively to this issue."[4]

By several accounts, the NCRG since its inception has funded the majority of problem gambling research in the country. One prominent researcher who has taken millions from the gambling group estimates that it funds the "vast majority" of such research conducted in the United States.[5]

Christine Reilly was the first executive director of the NCRG. She now serves in the same capacity with the Institute for Research on Gambling Disorders, the NCRG component that manages a research grants program. In an interview, Reilly also talked about how the gambling industry is anxious not to have its research efforts compared with those of the tobacco industry, the sponsor of "one of the worst public health disasters on earth."

Over the last decade and a half, the commercial casino industry has been on a relentless quest for research respectability. Under the reign of Reilly and the NCRG board of directors, the majority of whom are gambling industry officials, the nonprofit has issued large grants to researchers connected to Harvard and Yale and other prestigious medical schools. And it's enacted stringent rules to try to ensure the integrity of NCRG-funded research.

Research into problem and pathological gambling in the United States is at a crossroad. The American Psychiatric Association is in the process of altering the definition of pathological gambling, for the first time classifying the disease as a behavioral addiction akin to alcoholism or drug dependency, rather than an impulse control disorder like kleptomania. Scientists are increasing their understanding of how gambling affects the brain. Pharmaceutical companies are racing to put the first pill on the shelves to treat problem gambling.

And as I detail in the book's final chapter, Congress is moving steadily toward passing a bill that would provide an alternative to the industry's dominant stream of problem gambling research funding. In Canada, England, and Australia, national and provincial governments take the lead in funding research. Allowing our federal government to play a role is a step proponents say is vital to ensuring that the widest array of truly independent research about gambling and its addictiveness can be produced.

As three-quarters of the states are debating legalizing additional gambling, critics are questioning whether it's appropriate that the gambling industry is funding the majority of research into the topic in this country. The questions they're raising are pretty basic: Is there a fundamental conflict of interest in play when the industry is funding the bulk of the studies—many of which are being used to aid industry arguments to build new casinos and slot parlors across America? And, are there important issues not being studied because of the industry's dominant funding role, including topics that question whether casinos are aiming to extract a greater share of their profits from addicted gamblers?

The NCRG was Fahrenkopf's brainchild. A man with long Nevada ties, Fahrenkopf came naturally to his job at the AGA. He went to college at the University of Nevada, Reno, and after law school took a job with a Reno law firm. As his legal career grew, eventually taking him to a large firm in Washington, D.C., he simultaneously immersed himself in Republican Party politics. In 1983, he was installed as chairman of the Republican National Committee. He served for six years, through the end of President Ronald Reagan's second term.

In his 1996 speech, Fahrenkopf noted that the first issue he raised with the AGA's board when he agreed to take the post the year before was the necessity of acknowledging that problem and underage gambling were important issues.

"At that time, I was convinced that it is essential that the industry get ahead of the curve on the issue and recognize the importance of sending the message that we, as an industry, will take care of our own problems," said Fahrenkopf, who as of 2009 earned a $2 million annual AGA salary.[6] "I felt we must step to the plate, help identify the extent of the problem and then help find solutions that include not only treatment, but education and prevention."[7]

The AGA board agreed and authorized the NCRG's formation. The NCRG was first headquartered at the University of Missouri–Kansas City. It's now housed inside the same suite of offices as the AGA on Pennsylvania Avenue in Washington, D.C., a few blocks from the White House.

As of August 2010, the nine-member board of directors of the NCRG was composed of six top gambling industry executives, including officials with Harrah's Entertainment, MGM Mirage, and Boyd Gaming Corporation. The board chairman is Glenn Christenson, formerly the chief financial officer of Station Casinos, Incorporated. The board is rounded out with Bruce Shear, the CEO of a group of mental health, drug, and alcohol addiction treatment centers, which include two in southern Nevada, and Sue Cox, the founding executive director of the Texas Council on Problem and Compulsive Gambling.

According to its website, more than $22 million has been committed to the NCRG since its founding. In 2008, the three companies which gave the group the most were Harrah's, which contributed $400,000; MGM Mirage, which donated $286,000; and the country's largest slot machine maker, International Game Technology of Reno, which also produces gambling software and network systems. They gave $200,000.

It's clear that the founding of the NCRG reinvigorated the field of problem gambling research. Even most industry critics concede the point. Many important studies had been conducted into the origins of pathological gambling and the impact of the disease on gamblers in the two decades prior to the group's founding. But there had been relatively few peer-reviewed studies, the NCRG notes on its website, at least compared with the number undertaken after the group began doling out funds.

According to Reilly, NCRG-funded research has been conducted at thirty universities and has resulted in more than 170 scholarly articles published in well-regarded publications. Many of the studies have been path-breaking and have led the way in helping to determine the scope and parameters of problem gambling, she said.

The first study commissioned by the group was the meta-analysis of problem gambling studies conducted by Howard Shaffer, a professor at Harvard Medical School and director of what was then the medical school's Division on Addictions (the division is now part of Cambridge Health Alliance, a teaching affiliate of the medical school). As mentioned in the Introduction, Shaffer looked at 120 gambling prevalence research studies conducted in the United States and Canada between 1974 and 1997. While the studies conducted from 1977 to 1993 determined that at some point over their lifetimes, 4.38 percent of the two countries' general populations had become problem or pathological gamblers, the more recent studies showed a significant rise in the percentage of "lifetime" problem or pathological gamblers—to 6.72 percent.

This isn't the data the gambling industry touts from that groundbreaking study, however. As mentioned in American Gaming Association website fact sheets and in speeches by the group's leaders, the study also concluded that the more recent group of studies in Shaffer's survey had shown that 1.29 percent of American and Canadian adults in the past year had been active pathological gamblers, the most serious level of gambling addiction. This ignores the existence of more than twice as many past-year "problem" gamblers, what the study calls "Level 2" gamblers, who don't exhibit as many symptoms as pathological gamblers but who still, as Shaffer notes in the study, suffer from "a wide range of adverse reactions or consequences."[8]

Compared with the study of alcohol and drug addictions, problem gambling research is a young field. Though the first Gamblers Anonymous meeting took place in Los Angeles in 1957, research into gambling addiction didn't begin to really take shape until the early 1970s, when a psychiatrist named Robert Custer, director of a Veterans Administration addiction program in Brecksville, Ohio, established the first in-patient gambling treatment program. One of the first to recognize pathological gambling as a behavioral addiction, Custer believed addicted gamblers engaged in the activity primarily to escape pain. As opposed to nonaddicted, social gamblers, "the compulsive gambler usually goes alone. He's isolated. He's doing it to relieve some kind of psychic pain. Whether he wins or loses, just being in action relieves the pain," he said.[9] He died in 1990.

Henry Lesieur coauthored a seminal study on the topic with Custer in 1984, entitled "Pathological Gambling: Roots, Phases, and Treatment." He also wrote one of the first books on the topic. When the NCRG formed, they asked Lesieur, a psychologist currently with Rhode Island Hospital's gambling treatment program, to join an advisory board. He agreed, but soon after, he and another prominent gambling researcher, Richard Rosenthal, quit the board. According to media accounts, they left because of concerns about the industry's influence over the research it funded.[10]

In an interview, Lesieur said he split with the NCRG because of a misunderstanding regarding the role of the advisory panel members. He also suggested that credit should be given to the NCRG for providing the funds for a great deal of problem gambling research at a time when there were few funding sources available. What's more, he noted that some of the studies the group has funded have been accepted by top journals—and even cited by antigambling activists to support their cause.

Yet Lesieur remains skeptical about the role and mission of the NCRG. He doubts, for example, that they will ever fund research that concludes the casino industry stands to blame in any significant way for the addicted gamblers in their midst. Because of the industry companies that fund the research, the scientists who accept the grants are "only going to ask certain types of questions. It's *impossible* to ask certain types of questions because of that relationship," he said. That includes research into any casino programs or games that might spur addictive behavior such as slot and video poker machines. "It's just not going to happen because of who's on the board of the funding agency," he said, referring to the casino companies, slot machine makers and testing companies that dominate the NCRG board.

Little has been written about the NCRG and the apparent conflicts that stem from its role in problem gambling research funding. The *Los Angeles Times, Boston Globe,* and Salon.com published the only three stories I could find on the topic. They each raised concerns about the viability of gambling industry–funded research and questioned whether certain topics were under-studied, or not studied at all, because of the industry's dominance.

"While NCRG leaders say they fund independent science, it's not a coincidence that the science aligns so well with the interests of the casinos," concluded the Salon.com story. "It's not that gambling executives are tampering with research findings, or scientists are skewing results. Rather, gaming executives are drawing extravagant conclusions from the studies. By trumpeting these conclusions, the gaming industry is helping casinos gain a legal foothold across the country—and covering up the ways casinos profit from gambling addiction."[11]

The issue of the ethics of industry-funded research is not new. Nor is it unique to the gambling industry. Studies have shown that corporate-sponsored research in fields ranging from pharmaceuticals to household consumer goods is more likely to reach conclusions that favor the sponsor. The effects of industry financing, experts conclude, often lead to conscious and unconscious biases in the research.

Studies that are industry-funded make it significantly more likely that the "results will support the use of those products and services," said Eric G. Campbell, an expert on academic-industry relationships in biomedical research with the Mongan Institute for Health Policy. Campbell, a sociologist who teaches at Harvard Medical School, said in an interview that industry-funded research often affects everything from which proposals get funded, to how studies are designed, to what results get reported. It's in the interest of the industry to be publicly seen as supportive of research, he said—and then to control the questions asked and the outcomes reached.

Campbell said that if he was a top gambling industry executive, he'd want to find out the three best ways to reduce problem gambling. "Then, I'd find the least efficacious way to combat the problem of the three, and I'd support that," he said. Historically, the food, alcohol, and tobacco industries each have repeatedly used the strategy, he said. This approach gives the appearance that the industry is working hard to fight the problem, when in reality it's trying to minimize threats to its profit margins.

This is the theory of gambling critics: the casino industry created the NCRG to try to establish the idea that pathological gambling is caused by gamblers who mostly suffer from addictive "personalities." Under this theory, casinos and other gambling operators aren't responsible in any way for getting gamblers hooked. This not only aids the industry in its state-by-state legalization fights, but it establishes a ready-made defense against potential lawsuits.

Many NCRG-issued grants have been issued to studies that seek to figure out the genetic, neurological, and chemical causes of gambling addiction. Specifically, several research efforts have delved into how gambling affects the brain, including surveys into brain imaging and possible drug treatments. Some of the research has found links between gambling addiction and other addictions or "impulse control" behaviors. The theory is that pathological gambling is often just one manifestation of an addiction disease with "multiple opportunistic expressions." Shaffer calls this the "syndrome model,"[12] and claims that as many as three out of four pathological gamblers fall into that category (other researchers have concluded that just one in two pathological gamblers suffer from other addictions). Another NCRG-funded researcher, Dr. Jon Grant of the University of Minnesota, refers to a similar theory as the "susceptibility model" of pathological gambling. These ideas buttress the notion that most problem gamblers have addictive natures through which they're also psychologically predisposed to abuse alcohol or drugs or sex, etcetera.

A logical extension of this argument is that if the typical problem gambler couldn't express her addictive personality through buying lottery tickets or playing the slots—if those things weren't available to her—then she'd simply shop to excess, take addictive drugs, or find some other way to express her illness. Therefore, casinos can't be blamed for being around to nourish her addiction.

One way to cast doubt on gambling industry–funded research is to look at what's being studied, and how industry-funded researchers are trying to define the issue. Another way is to look at what they're not studying.

The gambling industry has not touched on many issues necessary to develop a well-rounded view of gambling addiction, its causes, or its consequences. Reilly confirmed to me that proposals that directly centered on the following topics have never been funded by the NCRG: Whether and how slot and video poker machines, including video lottery machines, are manipulated to be especially addictive. Whether gamblers addicted to these machines are more difficult to treat than other gamblers. Whether casino player reward programs, also known as player loyalty programs, likewise spur addiction and relapse. And, whether casinos and other gambling businesses generate the majority of their revenues from gambling addicts, as has been repeatedly estimated.

(Shaffer noted that some of the above issues have been mentioned in NCRG studies. But he did not contradict Reilly's confirmation that the NCRG had not funded studies that primarily investigated any of those four topics.)

Reilly also confirmed that there's a dearth of NCRG-funded research on another important topic: the impacts of pathological gambling on gamblers' families. In an e-mail, she noted two, including one study on the family histories of gamblers, conducted by researchers at the University of Iowa, which found that problem gamblers tend to have first-degree relatives, such as parents, who also have or had such problems. The NCRG also supported another study looking at couples' behavioral therapy for problem gamblers and their spouses, she wrote, but not enough subjects could be recruited to carry out the project.

On the same note, in combing through the websites of the NCRG, its affiliated institute, and the Division on Addictions, I found just a couple of studies the NCRG had funded that focused directly on the social costs of legalized gambling, including suicide. I found none at all that studied in detail the connection between problem gambling and other social costs such as bankruptcies, divorces, or gambling-related crime.

To be sure, state agencies, nonprofit groups, and foreign governments have funded studies on the above issues, with the possible exception of the impact of player reward programs. Critics say there's little mystery why the NCRG has not. Collectively, the results of such studies have the potential to cast casinos as businesses increasingly designed to mine as much money as they can from addicted gamblers, despite the ripples of pain that spread out from the addicts toward their families, friends, colleagues, and communities.

"They're not going to fund anything that's going to hurt them, or that has the potential to hurt them," said Joanna Franklin, a member of several committees of the National Council on Problem Gambling.[13]

There are other indicators that industry officials have worked behind the scenes to shape problem gambling research in their favor. Fahrenkopf himself commissioned research to discredit a groundbreaking and widely publicized 1997 study by a University of California, San Diego, sociologist and suicide expert named David Phillips.[14] Phillips concluded that suicide rates were significantly higher in gambling-intensive Las Vegas, Reno, and Atlantic City than they were in similar-sized cities that had no legalized gambling.[15] Perhaps predictably, the subsequent Fahrenkopf-sponsored study contradicted Phillips's conclusions[16] (and those of other scholars who have frequently found a strong link between pathological gambling and suicide).

Other casino heavyweights have made their displeasure known over studies they haven't liked. UNLV researcher William Thompson has written several papers on the social costs of legalized gambling, including the study on Las Vegas gamblers noted in an earlier chapter. According to Thompson, then-Mirage CEO Steve Wynn called him multiple times after the studies were released. More than once, Thompson said he picked up the phone to hear Wynn screaming profanities at him.[17]

Several years after its formation, the NCRG found a home at arguably the most prestigious medical school in the country. In 2000, the NCRG awarded Harvard Medical School's Division on Addictions a two-year, $2.4-million contract to establish the Institute for Research on Pathological Gambling and Related Disorders. The institute kept a portion of the funds for in-house research by Shaffer and his group, and distributed the rest in grants to researchers at other universities.

The arrangement came about when Fahrenkopf asked Shaffer if the industry could base its research effort there. Harvard Medical School administrators approved the plan, under requirements that the gambling industry not be allowed to review results of studies before publication. Further, the medical school insisted that scientists be allowed to publish whatever results they reached.[18] The arrangement was continued through several additional multiyear contracts until 2009, when the institute moved out of the Division on Addictions. By then, Shaffer's unit had separated from the medical school and moved to the Cambridge Health Alliance, a teaching affiliate of the school.

NCRG-funded research based out of Shaffer's thirteen-member research team at the Division on Addictions has included studies on everything including the incidence youth gambling, problem gambling relapse rates, addiction among Korean gamblers, and the drinking and gambling habits of casino employees.

When the institute moved out of the division's offices, its name changed slightly to the Institute for Research on Gambling Disorders. But the disaffiliation with Harvard only prompted the commercial casino industry to find other top American medical schools to connect themselves to. The same year the institute split with Shaffer's division, it created two new "NCRG Centers of Excellence in Gambling Research" to conduct large portions of its funded research. Psychiatrists with the medical schools at Yale and the University of Minnesota each received three-year grants totaling just over $400,000.

At Yale, according to the NCRG website, Dr. Mark Potenza is heading research into finding ways to treat pathological gamblers using a multidisciplinary approach, including psychopharmacological, brain imaging, and genetic responses. At Minnesota, Jon Grant is leading a team studying five hundred adolescents and young adults, aged thirteen to twenty-five, for a range of "impulsive" behaviors, from pathological gambling to reckless driving, sexual promiscuity, and excessive drug and alcohol use. Grant's "susceptibility model" thesis is that "identifying and understanding these commonalities of impulsivity may reveal the driving force behind pathological gambling."

It's clear from Shaffer's Division on Addictions online listing of his current and completed funded research, that he's focused mostly on one addiction, pathological gambling, but also has studied other addictions. According to the site, completed research funded by the NCRG resulted in more than sixty published studies. Since its disaffiliation with the NCRG, the division appears to be taking a greater percentage of grants from the National Institutes of Health (NIH), universities, local community foundations, and other nonprofits. But Shaffer's work is still being subsidized by the gambling industry. Its current research includes a project funded by bwin Interactive Entertainment AG, a huge, Austrian-based online gambling company with more than twenty million customers. Shaffer's project with bwin, entitled "Addiction and Technology: A Comprehensive Public Health Approach to Understanding the Internet and Internet-Related Disorders," has resulted in the publication of five studies to date.

Shaffer vehemently defends his research, including that which has been funded by the gambling industry. "I'm certainly not an apologist for the industry," he said in an interview. He said he understands the doubt about the industry's funding role in his and other scientists' research. "It's all healthy, proper skepticism," he said. But he said the fact is no one has ever tried to interfere with his research at any stage in the process. "I haven't felt pressure, and if I had, I would have walked the moment I felt it," he said.

Shaffer said accusations of bias can be rebutted by the fact that his published studies are peer-reviewed—a process in which an impartial panel of researchers knowledgeable about the same topic pore over a study offered for publication, to make sure its methods are rigorous, its conclusions are fairly reached, and personal bias has been avoided.

Shaffer arguably has written more than anyone on the issue of problem gambling prevalence nationwide. His various conclusions have been touted for more than a decade by many in different gambling legalization debates, but seemingly most often by the gambling industry to support its arguments. As mentioned, a close look at his 1997 meta-analysis showed a stark increase in problem gambling prevalence from the 1970s to the 1990s. But Shaffer was quick to note that subsequent research of his, and that of others, has showed that national prevalence rates have stopped rising since the late 1990s. He believes this is the case because many gamblers have adapted to their new environment. What happens is the most vulnerable are hit early, he said, and they develop immunities to their gambling addiction—if they survive. "What you see is adaptation to exposure," he said.

Shaffer's adaptation thesis is not universally accepted, among either American or foreign-based gambling researchers. A 2009 meta-analysis of thirty-four different problem gambling studies in New Zealand and Australia conducted since 1991, showed that with increased exposure to gambling, specifically to slot machines, there was a concurrent rise in problem and pathological gambling rates. Though they also found a very slight decrease in prevalence rates over time when the levels of machines held constant, their main conclusion was clear: with increased availability came increased addiction. "Strong statistically meaningful relationships were found for an increase in prevalence with increasing per capita density of [electronic gaming machines], consistent with the access hypothesis," the researchers concluded.[19]

Shaffer took issue with my conclusion that Las Vegas is a fundamentally distorted community in part because of gambling's complete immersion there. He also rejected the notion that the fast-rising number of Gamblers Anonymous meetings nationally has been the result of a rise in problem gambling.

Regarding Vegas, Shaffer argued that the most recent prevalence study conducted in Nevada showed lower problem gambling rates than what the data most plainly appear to show, or what the survey's author had concluded. He also noted the findings of that study found lower than average rates of youth gambling in Nevada. But here's what he neglected to mention: young Nevadans may gamble less, but they get into trouble at far higher rates than adults in the state: "In spite of the fact that older adults in Nevada do more gambling than younger adults . . . the prevalence of problem gambling is substantially higher among younger adults in Nevada."[20]

Regarding Gamblers Anonymous, Shaffer takes the position that the number of chapters has risen because of increased awareness of problem gambling, not because of an increase in problem gambling itself.

Before Shaffer received his doctorate in psychology in 1974, he worked for years as a freelance photographer in southern Florida for various news services and corporate clients. When his academic career picked up steam, he put down his camera. Relatively recently, the bug struck him again and he learned how to shoot with a digital camera. His personal photography website exhibits mostly color landscape shots he's taken during trips to western national parks, golf courses, China, Las Vegas, and elsewhere. His photos are well-composed and beautifully lighted. He has a precise and artistic touch.

Shaffer's main mission as a photographer has merged with his calling to bring exposure to his notion that various addictive behaviors are expressed through, as he puts it, "a common underlying biopsychosocial vulnerability." He's developed a photo essay project called *Expressions of Addiction: The Many Faces of a Syndrome,* which has shown everywhere from the Massachusetts State House to the Rio All-Suite Hotel and Casino just off the Las Vegas Strip. The gallery consists of black-and-white portraits of seventeen recovering addicts.[21] There are captions beneath the multiple photos of each person, which tell the story of their descent into addiction and their climb out. About half of those who agreed to be photographed suffer from more than one addiction—or as Shaffer would put it, from more than one expression of their addiction syndrome.

Most of the subjects are American, but one, recovering problem gambler Stanley W., is from China. He and Shaffer met at a Hong Kong treatment center. Stanley had accrued $100,000 in debt to family members after gambling on the stock market for fifteen years. Two years in recovery and debt-free, he told Shaffer: "My Chinese name . . . means happy forever. Before gambling it was who I was. . . . Now I am catching up."

Though she's become a media point person for the gambling industry, Christine Reilly doesn't have a background in the gambling world. Prior to joining the NCRG in 1997, she served as executive director of the Missouri Humanities Council, the state affiliate of the National Endowment for the Humanities. For that matter, she's said she doesn't like to gamble. "I play a slot machine for ten minutes, and I'm so bored I want to shoot myself," she said in a 2008 interview.[22]

The positions of Reilly and Shaffer often sound similar. Connecting a rise in the number of GA meetings to a concurrent growth in gambling availability is not scientific evidence, she told me. All it reflects is an increase in "treatment-seeking behavior" for addicted gambling and doesn't necessarily mean there's an increased prevalence of problem gambling. Like Shaffer, she also touts the adaptation theory in explaining why national problem gambling prevalence rates seem to have recently remained stable. And, as Shaffer has said regarding his syndrome theory, she advances the notion that "things" such as slot machines aren't inherently addictive; it's the relationship between the addiction-prone person and the thing, such as a slot machine, that might spur the addictive behavior.

Reilly said NCRG-funded research is as untainted as that funded by any other source. For starters, "there's no way that the industry can be involved with the outcome," she said. According to the NCRG's funding flow chart, neither the AGA's nor the NCRG's board of directors has any say in what grants are approved. A panel of researchers from the Institute's Scientific Advisory Board is assembled to evaluate each grant proposal. The criteria they use is modeled after the standards used by the NIH. On top of that, she noted, studies funded by her group have consistently been published in peer-reviewed journals.

When asked about various topics that NCRG-funded studies have not delved into, she minimized the need for research on player reward programs by equating them with department store sales. Regarding why the NCRG hasn't funded studies looking into pathological gambling's impact on families, she said the "horrible impact" on families is widely known. "Maybe scientists are more interested in other topics that don't have clear answers," she said.

Regardless, the reason Reilly said her group hasn't funded studies on one of the topics, the addictiveness of gambling machines, is that proposals on that topic haven't been submitted. (When I tried subsequently to clarify whether the NCRG had ever turned down research proposals on the other topics I asked about, or whether, instead, none had ever been submitted, Reilly responded by e-mail that despite her calls for proposed studies into problem gambling's social and economic impact, only one had been submitted, but it was not funded. Proposals do not get rejected because of topic, she said, but because of a lack of scientific merit.)

Reilly took note to defend Shaffer's reputation. "He's the best in the biz," she said. And despite the insinuations of gambling critics that the research coming from him or other researchers with the Division on Addictions is overly favorable to the gambling industry, she said "it'd be kind of hard to buy Harvard at $1 million per year." She added that despite the end of the contract between the Harvard-affiliated division and the NCRG, it didn't preclude the possibility that the NCRG could fund more individual division projects there down the road.

• • •

Cultural anthropologist Natasha Dow Schüll has been following the NCRG since its inception. Schüll, an associate professor at the Massachusetts Institute of Technology, is also an expert on the addictiveness of slot machines, having studied the topic for more than a decade. She said the industry's position unfairly ignores the way the designs of the machines can lend them addictive properties. "You can't ignore the way these machines are designed," she said. Instead of always looking at the gambler for being solely at fault for his addiction, "let's look at the machine side."

Schüll will soon be publishing a book called *Addiction by Design: Machine Gambling in Las Vegas*. In it, she'll be talking about how slot machines have a mechanical rhythm than can entrance gamblers into something she's heard them call the "machine zone," in which many gamblers play not necessarily to win large amounts, but rather to win enough simply to keep playing. In an interview, she pointed to what she called the "consumer protection model." Slot machines aren't treated as consumer products, she said, but if they were, there would be more of a burden on casinos and manufacturers to demonstrate their safety. Currently, she said, every consumer is potentially harmed by these machines.

"A natural consequence of interacting with these machines," said Schüll, is behavior that looks and often is addictive. "The industry is not necessarily trying to get players addicted, but they are trying to get them to play longer, faster, and more."

Schüll has also provided strong rebuttals to some of the most fundamental arguments of the gambling industry. For example, take just one of the research topics Reilly confirmed to me the NCRG has never funded—determining the percentage of casino revenues derived from problem and pathological gamblers. Industry officials including Reilly have dismissed the notion, either by claiming that studies on the topic have reached inflated conclusions, or by claiming that such research is of little worth because it's too difficult a measure to gauge. Yet this hasn't stopped many veteran researchers in the United States, Canada, and Australia from studying the topic, as Schüll notes in her upcoming book—and collectively reaching a conclusion that is damning to the industry. Seven studies published between 1998 and 2010 found that between 30 percent and 60 percent of casino revenues derived from less than 5 percent of the population classified as addicted gamblers. The highest revenue percentages consistently came from those problem gamblers who played slot or video poker machines.

Long before scientists began poking around problem gamblers' brains by studying neurological patterns and the like, a century ago psychoanalysts started coming up with a different series of answers about what prompted gambling addiction.

Sigmund Freud looked to literature for clues and found a great test case in Fyodor Dostoyevsky. The Russian writer was also a widely known inveterate gambler, and often got into big financial trouble because of his compulsion. In today's lingo, there's little question he'd be classified as a pathological gambler. Stories abound about how he repeatedly pawned his wife's jewelry and furniture to fund his gambling.[23] While in the middle of trips to casinos in German spa towns like Baden-Baden and Wiesbaden, he'd also sometimes gamble away his return fare to St. Petersburg, leaving him to write his wife to beg her to bail him out. Legend has it he was spurred to write some of his most famous books, including *Crime and Punishment,* because he'd been tapped out at the roulette tables he favored and needed more advance money from his publisher.

One of the main themes of Dostoyevsky's short novel *The Gambler* is the protagonist's adventures at the roulette wheel, largely based on his own casino experiences and observations. The gambling scenes are gripping and authentic, though of course if written today they would have to be updated for the 24–7 culture that exists in casinos all over the country: "After ten o'clock only the genuine, desperate players are left around the gaming tables, those for whom the only thing that exists at the spa is the roulette, and who have come for that alone, those who barely notice what is going on around them and who take no interest in anything throughout the whole season, who do nothing but gamble from dawn to dusk, and who would happily gamble through the night until daybreak if it were possible."

After learning about Dostoyevsky's gambling troubles, Freud came to the conclusion that gambling is masturbation, displaced. As he wrote to a friend, "[M]asturbation is the one great habit that is a 'primary addiction,' and that the other addictions . . . only enter into life as a substitute and replacement for it."[24]

Freud was also taken by Dostoyevsky's note to an acquaintance in which he talked about how he gambled more for the excitement of it rather than the need for money. Freud concluded that the writer's main quest, then, was the desire for "action." Further, Freud found that because Dostoyevsky's gambling often led to his destitution, gambling was a method of self-punishment. Both of these theories—that the problem gambler has a need to be in action, and that he has a deep-seated, perhaps unconscious desire to hurt himself—whether true or not, have become conventional wisdom among many gambling pundits. (Freud's belief that gambling serves as a metaphor both for self-gratification and self-punishment seems odd to me, but perhaps that's a subject for another book.)

David Newmark, a modern-era psychologist, reached a different conclusion: gambling often serves as an escape mechanism. Interpreting Newmark's beliefs, one writer put it this way: "Gambling therefore offers an easy escape from reality that, for some, is preferable to facing the 'existential void' they feel in daily life. Instead of learning more appropriate ways of dealing with it, those of us who cannot accept what life has to offer may find that the 'spiritual transcendence' we experience through gambling lends order and meaning to a chaotic, incomprehensible world which we feel powerless to control."[25]

Beginning in 1980, modern psychiatry radically redefined gambling addiction. In large part because of the work begun by Robert Custer in Ohio almost a decade before, the publication of the third edition of the *Diagnostic and Statistical Manual of Mental Disorders* (*DSM-III*) that year marked the first time pathological gambling was included. (The *DSM* is the American Psychiatric Association's influential and widely used handbook for mental disorders in the United States. It's updated periodically to reflect evolving thinking on how certain conditions should be defined.)

The inclusion of pathological gambling into the *DSM-III* resulted in a major evolutionary shift in how gambling addiction was seen by those in a wide range of fields, from doctors to judges, social workers to preachers. The condition began to be accepted by many as a medical disorder, as opposed to a moral failing or sinful transgression that stemmed from personal weakness. With the *DSM* listing, "at once the problems associated with it changed from vice to disease," wrote author and researcher Brian Castellani in *Pathological Gambling: The Making of a Medical Problem.*[26]

As the *DSM-III-R*, the *DSM-IV*, and the *DSM-IV-TR* were released, between 1987 and 2000, the definition of pathological gambling continued to evolve. But it remained classified as an impulse control disorder, akin to such conditions as pyromania or kleptomania, rather than as an outright addiction. Under the most recent definition, pathological gambling is described as "persistent and recurrent maladaptive gambling behavior" as indicated by five or more of ten symptoms, a few of which include preoccupation with gambling; the need to gamble increasing amounts of money to achieve the same effect; unsuccessful efforts to cut back or quit; and gambling as a way of escaping problems.

But just as the perception of problem gambling changed dramatically in 1980, another historic change is in the works. In February 2010, a *DSM-V* work group recommended that a new category of "behavioral addictions" be formed for the first time—and suggested that pathological gambling be included as the sole disorder on the list. In psychiatry, only disorders involving substances such as alcohol and drugs have been considered full-fledged addictions. This proposed change would put gambling addiction on par with them. Final publication of the *DSM-V* is slated for 2013.

"There is substantive research that supports the position that pathological gambling and substance use disorders are very similar in the way they affect the brain and neurological reward system," said Charles O'Brien, chair of the Substance-Related Disorders Work Group.[27] He noted that Internet addiction and sex addiction were considered for inclusion on the proposed behavioral addiction list but were rejected because of a lack of sufficient research data on the topics.[28]

The gambling industry, in the form of Reilly's Institute for Research on Gambling Disorders, used the panel's recommendation as an excuse to make a suggestion of its own—one that would effectively minimize pathological gambling if implemented. As noted above, in the current *DSM,* pathological gambling is defined as a "persistent and recurrent" behavior. There's a clear reason why. Repeated studies have shown that gambling addiction is difficult to treat, reflected by the fact that relapse rates for such gamblers are high.

In the institute's April 2010 monthly online column, Reilly noted that the "persistent and recurrent" description had been challenged by several studies. In one such review of five studies, she noted—authored by Shaffer and three other researchers from the Division on Addictions—the authors found no evidence to support the assumption that people cannot recover from disordered gambling. "Although the *DSM-V* Work Group has not proposed altering the 'persistent and recurrent' language, ample opportunities remain for consideration of such ideas as the *DSM-V* development project moves toward publication," she wrote.

•   •   •

The rush gamblers crave is the high that's felt when a bet is made, and sometimes when the gambler is just anticipating making the bet. Blood surges to the face. The mouth dries up. Concentration narrows as time seems to slow. The high is fleeting but is repeated as soon as the next bet is made. The feeling exists whether the bet is won or lost—but can spike when the gambler wins, especially if it's more than expected.

The experience has been compared to snorting a line of cocaine. It's undoubtedly an imperfect analogy, but for the last decade, researchers have used it to study how biochemical substances such as dopamine work in gamblers' brains. Dopamine is the neurotransmitter that helps assess rewards such as food. When we experience pleasurable things—anything from a tall glass of lemonade over ice to a slot machine win—dopamine neurons fire. They help the brain learn about pleasure, including predicting when the sensation might return.

Addicted gamblers are different from nonaddicted ones inasmuch as their dopamine systems are vulnerable, scientists believe. The first time pathological gamblers win, a huge dopamine rush can occur that gets planted in their memory. But when that happens, some researchers believe that gambling junkies, like cocaine addicts, develop reward systems that respond to pleasing stimuli differently than nonaddicts. A certain high level of reward has to be given for many addicted gamblers to continue to feel pleasure. Using an MRI scanner, neurologists in Hamburg, Germany, gauged the responses of twelve gambling addicts and twelve nonaddicts to a card guessing game. When participants picked the correct card, they won a euro (worth a little more than one U.S. dollar). The nonaddicts who picked the right card increased their blood flow to the ventral striatum, a portion of the brain heavy with dopamine receptors that measures rewards. Comparably, the addicted gamblers' brains had far less blood flow to the area—indicating they needed a prize much larger than a single euro to get excited.[29]

Researchers inadvertently made an important discovery several years back when a small but not insignificant percentage of Parkinson's disease patients reacted to a new drug by suddenly suffering from sustained episodes of pathological gambling and other disorders. Parkinson's depletes dopamine. The drugs originally used to treat the disease resupplied the brain with dopamine. But a newer class of Parkinson's drugs does something slightly different—they stimulate dopamine receptors. These new drugs are responsible for the odd side effects that have affected up to 15 percent of Parkinson's patients taking them.

The U.S. Food and Drug Administration has not yet approved any drug to treat pathological gambling. But given the potential market size—millions of adults in this country alone who could benefit—it would make sense to believe researchers are working on the issue. They are. According to a September 2010 check of an NIH website that serves as a registry of federally and privately supported clinical trials conducted around the world, thirty-two such trials were focused on pathological gambling treatments. Of those, fifteen had been completed and two more had been withdrawn.

Several trials looked into proposed behavioral remedies to gambling addiction. Most of those involved different types of talk therapies. Another fourteen trials have investigated the feasibility of using different types of drugs, with names like naltrexone, bupropion, acamprosate, and nalmefene.

Naltrexone and nalmefene appear to be two of the most promising. Primarily used to treat alcohol dependence, both drugs have proved more effective than a placebo in treating pathological gambling in three separate randomized clinical trials. Both are opioid antagonists. "Opioids regulate dopamine pathways in areas of the brain linked with impulse control disorders, and opioid antagonists block opioid receptors in these regions." That description comes from the NIH paperwork describing one ongoing trial to see if naltrexone can be used to treat impulse control disorders, including pathological gambling, among those who developed such disorders because they've been taking the Parkinson's-fighting drugs that have been causing addictive symptoms. The study is being funded by the Michael J. Fox Foundation for Parkinson's Research.

A different trial, unrelated to Parkinson's disease, is the NCRG-funded naltrexone study at Yale being led by Mark Potenza. The study will try to determine whether the drug is effective in a "real-world" clinical setting. It's expected to be completed in 2012.

It's increasingly important that research continues into all types of new problem gambling treatments because it's clear that the gambling industry remains busy at work finding novel ways to entice gamblers to spend more than they intend.

Slot machines play a big role here. More than a decade ago, casino moguls began recognizing that electronic gaming devices—from traditional slots to video poker, video keno, and bingo—needed to be better recognized as their biggest profit-drivers. They did this by granting slots a greater and greater amount of space on casino floors. As of 2005, there were 740,000 slot and video poker machines and electronic lottery outlets spread throughout the country—five times more than there were in 1990.[30] According to a *60 Minutes* report that aired in January 2011, the number of slots had risen to almost 850,000. Slots of different varieties are currently legal in thirty-seven states, according to the American Gaming Association. In one recent year, almost forty million Americans played a slot machine. On average, these machines take in more than $1 billion in wagers, most of which is paid back to the gamblers.[31] The rest, called the "hold," is what the casinos make. In 2003, North American casinos won $82 million from slot machine players—per day.

Given that they can be so easily designed to manipulate gamblers' emotions and drives, their potential seems almost limitless. Officials with International Game Technology, the country's largest slot machine maker, have made it clear that their goal is to stimulate gamblers into playing for longer periods of time. Their primary aim: "Make people want to sit there. Use sight and sound and everything at our disposal to get people's juices going."[32]

The cumulative effect is a stronger addictive pull, experts say. "No other form of gambling manipulates the human mind as beautifully as these machines. I think that's why that's the most popular form of gambling with which people get into trouble," said veteran gambling addiction researcher Nancy Petry of the University of Connecticut School of Medicine.[33]

Gary Loveman, CEO of Harrah's Entertainment since 2003, calls the mega-casinos on the Las Vegas Strip "slot boxes."[34] But slot design is just part of the picture. Customers need to get to the gambling hall in the first place to play the machines. Sometimes that means they need to be coaxed back in. Casino marketers have been refining their player reward programs to do just that.

The program at Harrah's set the standard. The casino giant's Total Rewards player loyalty program has a customer database of more than forty million players.[35] To analyze the data, Harrah's spends $100 million per year on information technology–related costs. Computer profiles are built on players that include what types of games they like to play, how much they bet, how long they play in a given session, where they like to eat and shop, and more. Through the program, customers of each of Harrah's fifty-two casinos are then sent targeted enticements by e-mail and regular mail to come back and play more. The program has driven gambling revenues to 80 percent of Harrah's $9 billion business.[36] The industry standard is 45 percent.

Loveman and his number-crunchers learned that elderly slot players lost more money to Harrah's than any other player demographic. They also discovered that 90 percent of Harrah's profits came from roughly 10 percent of its most devoted gamblers.[37] "Harrah's data suggests that addicted gamblers are providing a disproportionate share of all casinos' profits. Which raises an uncomfortable, if moot, question: What would happen to casino profits if the addicts were eliminated?" wrote Christina Binkley in *Winner Takes All: Steve Wynn, Kirk Kerkorian, Gary Loveman, and the Race to Own Las Vegas.*

Loveman, a Harvard Business School professor before he signed on with Harrah's, said that when he had chats with gamblers in his casinos, they often told him they were deeply unhappy. "You ask someone how they're doing, and in a casino, they say, 'Shitty,'" he said. "I didn't know how to have that conversation—I didn't know how to respond."[38]

He quickly found an answer. His response was to try to erase his customers' scowls through human interaction. By doing so, it would increase the chances they would stay and gamble more. When players stuck their Total Rewards cards into slot machines as they sat down, casino officials started tracking their losses in real time. If they were losing more than the odds suggested they should, a floor person would approach the gambler and give them a token gift. Employees were also put through a three-day training program to learn how to "deflect gamblers' misery with empathy," wrote Binkley, through scripted, "Have you had fun?" remarks that sometimes included tossing them a free meal or cash voucher.

It was simple. Beyond his computer-controlled slots and his finely engineered player rewards program, Loveman had learned that sometimes all that's needed to keep a gambler playing and losing longer is a friendly ear.

CHAPTER 7

A Federal Role,
and a Look Forward

More than once, Keith Whyte, executive director of the National Council on Problem Gambling, has found himself at odds with both sides. A powerful segment of the gambling industry has taken issue with the Comprehensive Problem Gambling Act, for example, a bill before Congress that Whyte and the council have energetically promoted. The measure would grant the federal government millions to fund research into problem gambling—effectively challenging the industry's dominant position as the funder of the majority of such studies conducted over the last decade. In an October 2010 interview, Whyte noted that there's "not a lot of communication" these days between his group and the American Gaming Association (AGA)—his previous employer—which has come out against the bill.

At the same time, Whyte has had frosty relations with some antigambling activists who claim he's insufficiently attentive to the dangers of legalized gambling expansion. Whyte said that, in fact, he's been forced to turn down donations from antigambling groups on occasion because they would have mandated he come out against certain legalization efforts.

Whyte said that the council has no restrictions on donations—except any strings that would force the group to act against its mission. He makes it clear to both sides that the council's charge as the chief national advocate for programs and services to assist problem gamblers must not be compromised. He lets potential funders know that he will not be pressured into violating one of the chief tenets of both the national council and its thirty-four state affiliates: that none of the councils come across as pro- or antigambling, per se, and none take positions on the gambling legalization fights spreading throughout the country.

"I have to make sure we're not bought and paid for" by pro- or antigambling interests, Whyte said. "We like to say, if we're getting flak from both sides, we must be doing something right. I've been surprised at how easy it's been to stay in the center." During his dozen years as executive director of the council, he noted he's had a few mentors who have helped guide him in the intricacies of the job. This makes sense, given that he was just twenty-eight when he took the post in 1998. Moreover, Whyte, unlike many of the state council directors, isn't a recovering problem gambler (he said he plays roulette only on rare occasion, meaning when he's not on work business, and plays for no more than $20 at a pop).

One of those mentors was Don Hulen, the cofounder of the Arizona Council on Compulsive Gambling, who died in early 2010. Hulen told him that as he charted the direction of the national council, whether it was through developing new programs for the states or implementing a congressional agenda, he always needed to keep one question in mind: is it good for the problem gambler? "Let that be your guiding star," Hulen told him.

A lot has rested on Whyte's shoulders. His tenure has coincided with huge leaps in revenues from commercial and Indian casinos and the number of states with lotteries; the influx of video lottery and slot machines into racetracks, bars, and other venues; as well as technological advances that pushed gambling onto the Internet and even cell phones. After graduating Hampden-Sydney College in 1992, where he concentrated in Asian history, Whyte worked a brief stint as a policy analyst with the Department of Health and Human Services before moving to the American Bar Association, where he was an assistant with the Individual Rights and Responsibilities section. From there, he was recruited to join the AGA in 1995, when the group was formed, as its first research director. As he compiled research on gambling topics that had been conducted to date, he found that there was a huge amount that wasn't known about problem gambling. He quickly came to the realization that problem gambling was the "big, overriding issue" the industry faced as it grew. When the opportunity came to lead a national group whose mission it was to help problem gamblers, in part by raising awareness about the issue, he jumped.

When Whyte took over as executive director, he basically needed to create an organization from scratch. At the time, the nonprofit group, based in Washington, D.C., had just part-time workers. His first year on the job, he had $60,000 in grant funding to work with. He's made a lot of progress. By 2010, the council's budget had grown tenfold to $600,000, and there were four full-time employees, including him, on the payroll. The two largest recent corporate donations were from the slot machine maker International Game Technology and Mohegan Sun, the large Indian casino in Connecticut, both of which contributed $60,000.

Over the last decade, Whyte said he and his board of directors made the decision to slowly change its focus. Whyte said the council has been steadily shifting away from helping the industry develop corporate gaming "responsibility programs," and moving toward advocacy on behalf of problem gamblers and potential problem gamblers, through bolstered prevention efforts. In part, this means recognizing problem gambling as a health issue. Toward that end, the council and its affiliates are beginning to work with state school systems and colleges to make sure problem gambling is one of the types of addictions that students can have addressed when in need of counseling. The council also will soon be starting its Risk Education for Athletes Project (REAP) to educate athletes, some of whom are college student-athletes, about the risks of excessive gambling.

Whyte believes that problem gambling prevalence nationally has been "trending up" in recent years, in part as a result of the explosion of legalized gambling. This certainly would seem to be reflected in the fast-growing number of calls to the toll-free National Problem Gambling Helpline—(800) 522–4700—the council provides for gamblers seeking help. In the decade of 2000 to 2009, the number of calls more than doubled, in fact, from 115,000 to 270,000. In a press release announcing that there had been 2 million calls to the help line during the ten-year period, he said one of the main reasons for the growth in calls was due to the efforts of gambling operators and state health agencies to publicize the number.

Whyte said he is eager for a new national prevalence study to be conducted on problem gambling. It was 1998, the year he started at the council, when the last such comprehensive study was conducted. It's his hope to start conducting annual surveys on three big topics, so that long-term trends regarding problem gambling can be more accurately determined. The first, of course, is the prevalence both of gambling and problem gambling among Americans. The second is gauging public opinion about gambling, and the third would be a survey of services for problem gamblers, including how many people are being treated by how many counselors, and the like.

Which leads back to the Comprehensive Problem Gambling Act. It's Whyte's hope to begin his annual survey regardless of the status of the bill. But clearly, the type of study he envisions—and so many others—could be aided by a new funding stream totaling in the millions of dollars per year. He said he's appreciative of the research efforts undertaken by the NCRG and other industry sources, but doesn't understand why the AGA and other industry groups haven't come on board as supporters of the bill. How could they not support the measure, he asked, "if they're truly interested in furthering problem gambling research in this country?"

Whyte said it's a big mistake to rely on the gambling industry to fund the bulk of the research. "The fact that they fund a major amount of research is good in the sense that research needs funding," he said. But it's also "a travesty," not only in the sense that the industry works from what he called "enlightened self-interest, but the scope of the issue demands so much more. Their spending is totally inadequate to the task."

The problem gambling act would amend the Public Health Service Act to include new programs run through the Substance Abuse and Mental Health Services Administration (SAMHSA) to research, prevent, and raise awareness of the harmful consequences of problem and pathological gambling. Among other things, SAMHSA, a division of the U.S. Department of Health and Human Services, provides grants for alcohol, illegal drug, and tobacco prevention and treatment programs.

The act would cost $71 million over five years—at about $14 million per year, the tiniest of slivers of the annual $3.55 trillion U.S. budget. At $10 million for each of the five years, the largest chunk would go toward funding problem gambling prevention and treatment programs sponsored by state, local, and tribal governments as well as nonprofit groups. Another $4 million per year would go toward funding a new "national program of research on problem gambling." Finally, $200,000 per year would kick-start a national public awareness campaign through promotion of public service announcements.

As Whyte and Tim Christensen, president of the Association of Problem Gambling Service Administrators, have noted, not a single cent of that $3.55 trillion budget currently is dedicated to problem gambling—and not a single federal employee has problem gambling as part of their job responsibility or listed in their job description.

This is the case despite the fact that the federal government, through SAMHSA, spent $2.5 billion in 2010 alone on programs relating to the prevention and treatment of the abuse of substances such as alcohol, tobacco, and illegal drugs, according to the agency's website.[1]

Moreover, the feds completely ignore problem gambling prevention and treatment despite the fact that they profit handsomely from legalized gambling. They may not run lotteries directly as the states do, but the IRS collects $6 billion per year from a withholding tax on gambling winnings. Whyte and Christensen argue strenuously that this gives the federal government a responsibility to set aside a small portion of those federal gambling winnings—a miniscule portion, really, coming to just over two-tenths of 1 percent—to try to minimize the damage gambling can do.

Largely through the efforts of the national council, momentum for the problem gambling act has picked up in Congress. In their first two attempts, supporters were able to persuade only eight and ten U.S. House members respectively to sign on as cosponsors. But they persisted, and the bill was introduced again in June 2009. This time, they made it much further in the process. During the first nine months of 2010, Whyte said he and a team of national council grass-roots lobbyists have met with officials from 278 House offices and 76 Senate offices. By October 2010, 72 House members agreed to become cosponsors, and the bill was introduced for the first time in the U.S. Senate, where 4 cosponsors also have signed on. The measure has picked up bipartisan support in both chambers, though Democratic cosponsors outweigh Republicans by about a four-to-one margin.

Several of the Democratic House cosponsors pack important symbolic weight. As Las Vegas–area House members, Nevada Congresswomen Dina Titus and Shelley Berkley, as might be predicted, are outspoken supporters of the commercial casino industry. But both are also cosponsors of the act, as is Representative Barney Frank (Mass.), the lead sponsor of a bill to regulate online gambling.

Some gambling industry officials, as well as Howard Shaffer, the Harvard-affiliated researcher, have noted that government-funded research can be just as potentially problematic from a conflict-of-interest standpoint as is research sponsored by an industry group. Whyte said that's not the case in this instance because the federal government has no role in operating gambling facilities, and only a limited role in regulating any form of gambling, through the National Indian Gaming Commission (NIGC). (Whyte's first assertion is not 100 percent accurate, inasmuch as the four main branches of the U.S. military operate several thousand slot machines on overseas bases, a topic I go into later in this chapter.)

According to Whyte and Christensen, the federal government needs to follow the lead of many of the states that, to varying degrees, recognize that because they're profiting from an addictive activity they sanction, they owe a responsibility to those who have gotten hooked, and they likewise need to try to prevent others from developing problems. Since 2001, the number of states that offer at least some funding for programs to prevent and treat problem gambling has grown almost three-fold, from thirteen that year to thirty-eight in 2010, according to Christensen's group. Still, other data suggest the amount of public funds devoted to problem gambling services at the state level—a total of $13.5 million in 2010, about half of which goes to programs that subsidize treatment programs—is relatively small. Only fifteen states fund one or more full-time workers to manage the programs. The average per capita spending on such programs is 33 cents.

Moreover, the plunging economy caused reductions in these programs in ten states, Christensen estimates, including in Nevada, which I mentioned in an earlier chapter. This has happened intentionally, in cases like Nevada's where governors or legislators have decided that the small amounts used to assist problem gamblers is needed more to plug other parts of the budget. In other cases, the programs are funded as a function of gambling revenues, so when state taxes from gambling dry up, so does the percentage set aside to address problem gambling.

"From my perspective, the primary impact on these budget reductions is a loss of momentum for the services. Being a still relatively new field, the public in general has very low awareness not only of problem gambling as a disorder, but also how and where to access services when needed," said Christensen in an e-mail. "Public awareness and prevention activities are typically grossly underfunded to begin with, and when cuts or reductions occur, those are the activities that typically are eliminated first. So, while a state may have a wonderful treatment program, if those who are in need of it are not aware it exists, it becomes a problematic situation."

Whyte said he's encountered another, more disturbing trend: officials in some states, concerned that new prevalence studies might show possible rises in state-wide problem gambling rates after gambling has been legalized, are deliberately attempting to scuttle such studies. He decried the "breathtakingly cynical way they're chasing revenue without looking at the long-term costs."

All the more reason, Whyte has concluded, that it is time for the federal government to step in. He recognizes it won't be easy to pass the bill. More than two centuries of inertia on the issue need to be overcome. But he's prepared for a long fight if necessary. "This really is history we're trying to make," he said.

Given the ever-increasing amounts the gambling industry spends on Capitol Hill in lobbying efforts and campaign contributions, Whyte, Christensen, and company might be facing a tough task. In the 2008 election cycle, the casinos/gambling industry, as categorized by the nonpartisan Center for Responsive Politics in Washington, D.C., spent $17 million in campaign contributions to federal candidates and political action committees, more than it ever had before. That's a whopping thirty-five times the amount the industry spent on such contributions in 1990.[2] The three top contributors in 2008 were commercial casino companies MGM Mirage, Harrah's Entertainment, and Station Casinos, which spent a combined $2.5 million.[3] Rounding out the top five were two Indian tribes with casinos, the Viejas Band of Kumeyaay Indians and the San Manuel Band of Mission Indians. Almost 70 percent went to Democrats, consistent with the industry's tilt during the past two decades, according to the center. In the 2008 cycle and through October 2010, Senate Majority Leader Harry Reid of Nevada received more from the industry than any other politician or PAC.

The industry also has been spending more on federal lobbying campaigns. In 1998, they spent about $12 million. By 2009, the amount had risen to $26 million. During the first ten months of 2010, the top two lobbyists were Harrah's and the Interactive Gaming Council (IGC), a trade group of online wagering companies. Between the two, they spent about $1.8 million. Though Harrah's has had a broader mission than just lobbying for Representative Barney Frank's online gambling regulation bill, that recently has been a big part of their mission. Harrah's and other land-based casino companies including MGM Mirage have been eyeing ways into online gambling, and are expected to try to jump into the market if and when a bill like Frank's is passed. The AGA has taken a neutral stance on online gambling, however, because some of its prominent members, including Wynn Resorts, are against legalization and regulation of online casinos.[4] Harrah's, owner of the World Series of Poker, is especially interested in the possibility of expanding online, and in 2009, registered to lobby the federal government for the first time. The company spent just over $400,000 in the first three months of that year to lobby on behalf of Frank's bill.

Casino companies generally do not lobby Congress regarding expansion issues—those matters are left to the states. But they are interested in a range of other types of federal issues, including things like money laundering and corporate taxes, tourism and indoor air quality, and a range of labor issues that might affect businesses with tens of thousands of employees.

The gambling industry is wielding its influence at the state level to at least the same degree. In a July/August 1997 investigation, *Mother Jones* magazine found that the gambling industry had made contributions of more than $100 million to state politicians from 1992–1996. As gambling legalization fights since then have spread to almost every state, there can be little doubt that that number has risen sharply.

With money and influence sometimes comes corruption. That's certainly been the case with the gambling industry, historically anyway. When the late, well-respected Democratic senator Paul Simon of Illinois addressed the National Gambling Impact Study Commission, he stated that gambling "has more of a history of corruption than any other industry."[5] Remember, lottery corruption scandals brought down the first two waves of gambling in America. Fast-forward to a more recent time, the 1990s, when repeated legalized gambling-related corruption charges sprouted across the country, and it's easy to conclude Simon may have been right.

In Kentucky, a bribery investigation involving the state's horse racing industry resulted in convictions of fifteen state legislators. After escaping convictions in previous corruption trials, former Louisiana governor Edwin Edwards was convicted on charges that he extorted hundreds of thousands of dollars from businessmen applying for riverboat casino licenses. And in Arizona, eleven state legislators were indicted after a yearlong undercover operation in which they were caught on videotape promising to vote for legislation that would have legalized casinos after receiving cash.[6]

Frank Fahrenkopf Jr. has been the most prominent face of the legalized gambling industry since the mid-1990s. The commercial casino industry accounts for 37 percent of all legalized gambling revenues, according to a 2007 count from Fahrenkopf's group, the AGA, making it the largest segment of the industry. Indian casinos and state lotteries make up 28 percent and 27 percent, respectively. But over the decade and a half he's been in charge, Fahrenkopf has been more publicly visible on a variety of gambling-related political and social issues than any one official with groups representing Indian casinos or lotteries—not to mention much more active, through the National Center for Responsible Gaming, in sponsoring the majority of the country's problem gambling research.

Soon after Fahrenkopf took over at the AGA, Howard Shaffer's gambling prevalence study was released in 1997—the meta-analysis I referred to in the Introduction that noted a significant rise in problem and pathological gambling rates between an older time period and a more recent period in the 1990s. The AGA issued a press release in which Fahrenkopf, by today's standards, made what seems like a surprising concession. "The study basically confirms what common sense tells us," he said. "With the growth of all types of gaming all across the country, more people are gambling, and that growth has resulted in a small increase in problem gambling, but it is not related to any one form of gaming."[7]

These days, Fahrenkopf makes no such allowances. In a September 2010 phone interview, he said people are generally predisposed to a gambling addiction or they aren't—and that prevalence studies suggest the vast majority, 99 percent of the populace, aren't.[8] "Everyone accepts" that about 1 percent of the population are pathological gamblers, he said, and no more. "It's not availability, not proximity" that causes problem gambling, he said.

When he joined the AGA, Fahrenkopf said "we knew we had an obligation to do everything we could" to assist problem gamblers. "No one knew the proper way to treat people." He said that when the NCRG was created, critics claimed the industry was paying for its own results. But that's why stringent firewalls have been put in place to make sure that the research remains untainted by its funding source. "We've had to prove ourselves," he said, and have been vindicated by the peer-reviewed research "and the quality and reputation of the folks associated with the NCRG."

Fahrenkopf reiterated the gist of the statement sent to me by an AGA spokeswoman regarding why the group was against the Comprehensive Problem Gambling Act. He called it "really poorly drafted" and said additional federal bureaucracy would need to be created to implement the bill. What's more, it's unclear what types of programs would be created and where the federal funding ultimately would go, he said. He rejected the notion that the main reason the AGA is opposed is that the casino industry would have less control over what types of research topics would be studied or how the results might be interpreted.

When I asked Fahrenkopf about the 2010 poll conducted by the Saint Consulting Group, which showed that 72 percent of Americans were against a casino being built in their community—and that, of more than a dozen different types of developments only landfills were less popular—he called the survey "total, unadulterated bullshit." He also suggested that the 2006 debate in Cleveland with the Reverend Tom Grey, in which he said he would work "very, very hard" to stop a casino from being built in his own neighborhood, was a partial thought. He said because he lived in a residential neighborhood, he wouldn't want several types of retail establishments to plant themselves there.

Fahrenkopf said casinos were popular developments. He noted Iowa as an example. When casinos are legalized in an Iowa county, state law mandates that referendums be held every eight years by voters in that county, to make sure voters still want them to be legal. The referendums recently have gone the industry's way. In 2002, the casinos won in all eleven counties that voted and averaged 74 percent approval.[9] In 2010, voters in the counties with the state's seventeen casinos each said yes again, this time by a 78.5 percent margin.

Two issues seemed to irk Fahrenkopf more than any other: how the faltering economy could affect the gambling industry down the road, and the notion that legalized casinos are more of a long-term economic drain on a community than a boon. The claim regarding casino economics is "absolutely and totally false," he said. He called the three researchers he's gone up against in state legislative battles, Earl Grinols, John Kindt, and Robert Goodman, "the circle of disinformation." His voice rising, he said none of their arguments stand up.

He said he could not predict how the economy would affect the casino business in the future. "I couldn't tell you what's going to happen twenty years from now, let alone two months from now," Fahrenkopf said. That said, he doesn't think a saturation point has been reached for casinos. There's plenty of room for more. Only the marketplace will suggest when it's time to slow expansion efforts, he said. But that time hasn't yet come. "We'll know when the market tells us," he said, using Starbucks as an analogy. The coffeehouse chain suffered a modest contraction in 2008 after decades of unrelenting expansion. "When we see places closing down, then we'll know."

As Arkansas became the forty-third state in the modern era to institute a lottery, the state's nine-member lottery commission took some flak when it recruited South Carolina's lottery director and paid him $324,000 a year, a 49 percent increase over his previous salary.[10] The commission also hired two of the director's South Carolina deputies and paid them $225,000 each. But any concerns were washed away soon after the Arkansas Scholarship Lottery sold its first tickets in September 2009. Managers predicted they'd be seeing about $1 million in revenues per day. Instead, the state has been winning $1.4 million daily. When fiscal year 2010 ended in June, the state had taken in $380 million in winnings. The money funded 28,000 college scholarships ranging from $2,500 to $5,000 each. Yet only 22 percent of lottery revenues have gone toward the scholarships. The rest was paid out in prize winnings and office overhead, including salaries.

Just as the soured economy has boosted efforts for more casinos, state lotteries have done extremely well, at least through 2008. This is vital for state governments, which still earn more from lottery revenues than winnings from casinos or racinos. From 1993 to 2007, in fact, lottery proceeds to states, including revenues from video lottery terminals, doubled, from $8.8 billion to $17.7 billion.[11] Though revenues grew almost every year during that period, the growth slowed in the later years. Reports of lottery sales in 2008 to 2009 have been conflicted. According to one newspaper report, which relied on statistics gathered from a scratch-off lottery ticket manufacturer, from July 2008 to January 2009, twenty-five of the forty-two states that then had lotteries experienced higher sales of scratch-off tickets and daily lottery games. Yet another report, from the Nelson A. Rockefeller Institute of Government, concluded that from fiscal 2008 to 2009, lottery revenues in forty of the forty-two states where data were available declined by $349 million, or 2.3 percent.

Of the forty-three states that offer lotteries, twenty-four target some or all of the proceeds toward education. According to a 2007 *New York Times* study, in the states that use the money for schools, lotteries accounted for less than 1 percent to 5 percent of the total revenue for K-12 education.[12] Instead, the report found that the preponderance of the money raised by lotteries was used to sustain the games themselves, including marketing, prizes, commissions to vendors, and of course overhead. Over the years, nearly each of the states had increased payouts, in some cases though larger prizes, and decreased the amounts that went toward programs. And lotteries were offering an increasing number of games that offered instant gratification—including scratch tickets and video lottery terminals—that experts believe are inherently more addictive.

States in recent years have, in fact, been doing more to ensnare more "core" players, lottery officials in several states have said. Though they make up only 10 percent to 15 percent of lottery ticket buyers, they account for 80 percent of sales.[13] In fact, it would seem many of these players can't afford to make gambling a regular expenditure. Repeated studies have shown that lottery ticket buyers skew toward poorer Americans—and that lotteries, which advertise disproportionately in poorer neighborhoods, know this. A 1999 investigation from a Pittsburgh newspaper, for example, found that in Allegheny County, which includes Pittsburgh, "stores in neighborhoods with per capita income lower than $20,000 sold more than twice as many tickets per resident as those in neighborhoods where average incomes exceeded $30,000."[14] And almost 40 percent of the so-called "heavy," at-least-once-a-week players reported annual income below $25,000.

State lotteries spend hundreds of millions of dollars per year in advertisements. Many of the ads claim huge winnings may be right around the corner for you, but that win or lose—and of course the overwhelming likelihood is that you will lose—the money is put to noble use. But this has put governments in an awkward position, wrote Robert Goodman in *The Luck Business,* as lottery managers are not only trying to increase the amount of money people gamble, they're attempting to get people to alter their spending habits away from consumer goods and toward the lottery. "In this new promotional role, government finds itself in a strange and contradictory position which makes it difficult to carry out its role of protecting the public," he wrote. "While it once regulated gambling in order to guard against gambling operators who might take advantage of its citizens, the government's own growing dependence on gambling revenues puts pressure on state officials to increase advertising and relax regulations."[15]

Soon after New Hampshire started its lottery in 1964, many in the nation's Indian tribes began thinking, If the states can sanction and profit from gambling, why, as sovereign entities, can't we? Within a decade, after the U.S. Supreme Court found that states could not tax or regulate the activities of Indians on Indian reservations, a number of tribes opened bingo halls to raise revenues. But legal squabbles broke out with a number of states when the Indian gambling operations started to exceed state betting limits and other gambling regulations. A number of such cases wended their way through the federal courts, leading the U.S. Supreme Court to again address the matter in 1987. In *California v. Cabazon Band of Mission Indians*, the court sided with the tribe, ruling that, as governments, federally recognized tribes had the right to run gambling operations without interference from the states.

This set the stage for Congress to act, which they did a year later. The Indian Gaming Regulatory Act (IGRA) reaffirmed the principles of "tribal economic development, tribal self-sufficiency, and strong tribal government," established three classes of Indian gambling, and also set up the NIGC to regulate the new ventures. Class III establishments, which allowed the equivalent to high-stakes, full-service casinos, can have any type of gambling game that's legal in any capacity in the state. The congressional act also mandated that to open a casino, tribes had to sign an agreement with the state in which it's located, called a "compact." Though the compact requirement has spurred scores of court fights between different tribes and states, Indian gambling has mushroomed since the law was passed. According to the National Indian Gaming Association's 2009 Economic Impact Report, that year, 237 Indian tribes in twenty-eight states grossed $26.2 billion in revenues from their gambling operations.[16] They also earned a little more than $3 billion in related hospitality and entertainment ventures, including hotels, restaurants, and golf courses. The businesses created 628,000 direct and indirectly related jobs, the group found, and also generated more than $11 billion in tax revenues and regulatory payments to the federal and state governments.

According to testimony National Indian Gaming Association Chairman Ernest Stevens Jr. gave before the Senate Committee on

Indian Affairs in July 2010, gambling revenues fund "essential tribal government services" that include schools, health clinics, police and fire agencies, water and sewer services, and child and elderly care centers. Gaming revenues also have helped tribes to diversify their economies into businesses such as renewable energy and manufacturing, he said.[17] Yet tribes have had varying levels of success translating the success of their gambling businesses into sustained economic development for tribal members. In part, this is because not all Indian casinos have been equally successful. According to a 2000 Associated Press computer analysis of unemployment, poverty, and public assistance records, of the more than 130 tribes with casinos, "a few near major population centers have thrived while most others make just enough to cover the bills."[18]

The tribes also have had mixed success in terms of their responses to problem gambling. Just as different commercial casino companies have various policies regarding how extensively they train employees regarding problem gambling, what types of self-exclusion programs they offer, if any, and how much they may or may not choose to donate to the state or national problem gambling councils or other groups like the NCRG to support research, Indian casinos are the same way. It's really up to the casino, its top managers, and tribal leaders. Most at least do the minimum, including some training for their employees and posting a toll-free problem gambling help line number near casino entrances and cages and ATMs, measures that are sometimes proscribed through their compacts with the state.

There are tribes, including some in Washington state, where I've written about the topic, that offer free or reduced-cost counseling to anyone who gambles at their casino and has developed an addiction problem. Some tribes also offer self-exclusion policies that, at the problem gambler's request, prohibit the gambler from setting foot on the property again, under a legally enforceable threat of imprisonment. I know of at least one tribe in Washington that offers such a policy. (Various states and commercial casino chains around the country have experimented with self-exclusion policies, with mixed success.)

In general terms, some Indian gambling experts suggest that tribes take more of an interest in the issue of problem gambling than commercial casinos for a couple of reasons. First, Indian casinos represent individual tribes, which are keen on being seen as responsible members of the community. Also, tribe members work and gamble in Indian casinos, and the last thing tribal leaders want is to create new addicts among a population—their own population—who have suffered unduly from other types of addictions. "In general, tribes have a strong commitment to responsible gaming because tribal gaming facilities are within their communities," Dr. Kate Spilde, chair of the Sycuan Institute on Tribal Gaming at San Diego State University, told the publication *Tribal Government Gaming* in 2010. "The social expectations for tribal government are higher than they are for state and local governments. Since tribal gaming is established with a social purpose—to drive development and recovery—tribal leaders know it is important to acknowledge the potential problems associated with introducing a gaming facility into the community and to take measures to address those problems."[19]

To be sure, gambling addiction problems have resulted from the proliferation of Indian casinos. That includes tribe members, many of whom had never before been exposed to casino-style gambling. Gambling addiction is causing a range of new social problems on reservations and elsewhere in "Indian country," wrote Tim Giago, the former editor and publisher of *Lakota Times* and several other Indian publications, in 2005. These social problems include everything from leaving children at home alone to gambling away their paychecks or the "per capita" payments tribe members are paid from Indian casino winnings.[20]

"Although the casinos have turned out to be the goose that laid the golden egg to many heretofore poverty stricken tribes, their very success has created a new generation of gambling addicts," Giago wrote. "It is a shame to see the casinos grow at the expense of tribal members. Those dedicated groups and organizations on the Indian reservations that have so successfully fought alcoholism and drug addiction now have a new battle on their hands."

More recently, further evidence made its way to light regarding the after-effects of Indian casinos. In Oklahoma, experts believe the more than one hundred tribal casinos opened in the state have been the main cause in the apparent spike in problem gambling among state residents. From fiscal year 2007 to 2009, according to the Associated Press, the number of people who called the state's problem gambling help line grew from 627 to 912. During the same time period, the number of people seeking treatment for gambling addiction at one state-funded facility rose from 149 to 350.

The federal government does not run a lottery or federally operated, Las Vegas–style casinos. But there are some within the federal bureaucracy who run their own mini-slot machine parlors. The Pentagon operates several thousand slot machines on U.S. military bases abroad. The revenues raised—$130 million per year at last count— goes toward recreation programs for the troops, including movie theaters, concerts, and swimming pools. They also allow some lucky troops returning from Iraq and Afghanistan to take discounted trips to places like Disney World and luxury resorts in Hawaii.

According to a 2007 CNN story,[21] there were three thousand slot machines posted at Army and Marine bases, bringing in revenues of $130 million. The number of machines in Air Force and Navy facilities wasn't immediately disclosed. In 1999, the last time complete numbers were made available to the public, the Pentagon confirmed that it ran eight thousand slot machines on ninety-four overseas bases and posts. (The Army also runs bingo games on U.S. bases, which are comparatively modest, profiting the military at least $7 million annually.)

Critics say the premise of the program—taking money from troops to fund entertainment—is disgraceful. What's worse is that young soldiers, often competitive risk-takers by nature, are at higher risk for developing gambling problems. John Kindt of the University of Illinois, who has studied the issue, has said that about 2.2 percent of military personnel indicate in surveys that they are probable pathological gamblers, significantly higher than the percentage of adult Americans. "The military should not be a predator on its own soldiers and their families," he said. "To be a predator of their own people that are serving their country is outrageous."[22]

In a statement, an undersecretary of defense said the machines provide "a controlled alternative to unmonitored host-nation gambling venues and offers a higher payment percentage making it more entertainment oriented than that found at typical casinos."

The CNN story centered around Aaron Walsh, a decorated Apache helicopter pilot with the Army who became addicted to the slot machines he found on bases in Germany and South Korea. He received treatment through the military's only gambling treatment facility in Camp Pendleton in California, but it didn't take. He was kicked out of the military in 2005. A year later, after a visit to a casino in Bangor, Maine, he killed himself.

Several years before, Congress became sufficiently concerned about the effects of the on-base slot machines that they ordered the Pentagon to study how the machines were affecting military families. The final report provided no new data about problem gambling rates.[23] Instead, it warned Congress that the military would not be able to maintain programs like golf courses and family activity centers without slot machine revenues or another way to raise the same amount of cash.

In 2006, the gambling treatment facility at Camp Pendleton was shut down. Two years later, a bill sponsored by a Tennessee congressman to do away with the military's slot machines died in committee.

•　　•　　•

The largest segment of committed antigambling activists typically have come from socially conservative Christian denominations, including the Southern Baptist Convention and other evangelical churches. They believe gambling violates biblical principles, if not directly in letter than certainly in spirit. According to the gambling issue webpage from the Baptist Convention's Ethics and Religious Liberty Commission: "The Bible indicates that man is to work creatively and use his possessions for the good of others (Eph. 4:28); gambling fosters a something-for-nothing attitude. The Bible calls for careful stewardship; gambling calls for reckless abandon. The Bible condemns covetousness and materialism (Matt. 6:24–34); gambling has both at its heart."[24]

If there's any Christian group even more fundamentally opposed to gambling, it's the Church of Jesus Christ of Latter-day Saints, more commonly known as the Mormon Church. "Gambling is motivated by a desire to get something for nothing," reads the church's website. "This desire is spiritually destructive. It leads participants away from the Savior's teachings of love and service and toward the selfishness of the adversary. It undermines the virtues of work and thrift and the desire to give honest effort in all we do." The site makes it clear that church members are to be encouraged to become politically active in opposing "the legalization and government sponsorship of any form of gambling."[25] This steadfast antigambling stance is why Utah, home to the largest concentration of Mormons in the country, is one of two states without any legalized gambling— and why it likely will stay that way long after Hawaii succumbs.

(Other faiths prominent in American life, including more liberal, mainline Protestant denominations, such as the United Methodist Church and the Presbyterian Church, as well as Islamic religious groups, also take firmly antigambling stances. The Catholic Church and most Jewish denominations generally take less of a clearly negative view of gambling, though both warn about its addictive dangers.)

Beyond spiritual and Biblical considerations, religiously inspired gambling opponents most often refer to the human toll of addictive gambling—how gamblers themselves, their families, friends, and whole communities become disrupted by gambling through social costs such as crime and family neglect. This is where they find common cause with social activist liberals, many of whom have become outraged at what they believe is the gambling industry's predatory nature, and the vulnerability of those often seen as targeted most directly, the poor and the addicted. What's especially galling to many progressives is the fact that in the case of lotteries, private industry isn't to blame at all—it's the state that's intentionally adding to the misery of some of its least upwardly mobile citizens through advertising campaigns aimed at poor neighborhoods.

Many of the coalitions built in state after state against gambling expansion have been of this "strange bedfellows" variety—church-inspired objectors from the political right joined by community and religious activists from the political left.

Enter the Reverend Tom Grey, the most influential antigambling activist over the last two decades. A Methodist minister and Vietnam War infantry captain, Grey feels equally at home quoting both scripture and battlefield metaphors—with references to Martin Luther King Jr. and even *Rules for Radicals* author and community organizer Saul Alinsky thrown in for good measure. He bridges that strange bedfellows divide perfectly.

On a mission to stop gambling's spread since 1991, Grey has testified, lobbied, and organized in every state in the union save one, Wyoming, as well as in Australia, New, Zealand, and England. He was days away from turning seventy when I spoke with him in October 2010.

A Midwestern kid who played football at Dartmouth, Grey found the ministry in the late 1960s, after coming home from the war. He preached at a couple of different Chicago-area churches before being transferred to Galena in the northwest corner of Illinois. It was there, in 1991, when he picked up a newspaper to see a story about a county board vote to bring in a riverboat casino nearby. He went to the next board meeting, and when he raised objections, he was told about the painless revenues gambling could bring, that it would attract tourist gamblers instead of locals, and that it was a sound economic development plan for the region. Most folks at the meeting didn't seem to have objections.

"This is such a threat that it takes people and they buy this BS," he told me. Soon after, residents started changing their minds. More than 80 percent of the town residents voted in a nonbinding referendum against planting the boat in their community—but local officials allowed it to dock anyway. He was hooked on the topic soon after the incident.

He fought other gambling ballot initiatives in Illinois and won. Local activism turned national after he started getting calls from folks around the country similarly outraged that politicians were inviting gambling to take root in their cities, and that it seemed little could be done to stop them. In 1993, he created the National Coalition Against Legalized Gambling. Raising awareness is everything, he's found. "It's a battle in which every time you stand up and fight, you win. Whether you lose or win, you win," he said.

Several years ago, Grey changed the name of his organization to the Stop Predatory Gambling Foundation. It was a perception issue. The old name "gets you on ground you didn't want to fight on. They could try to pin us down as prohibitionists, which they did." Grey said he isn't a prohibitionist; he isn't looking to tear down the Las Vegas Strip, for example. But the unceasing spread of gambling into communities that don't want it, promoted by politicians using false arguments of economic salvation, is causing increased addiction and social costs that cannot be worth whatever modest tax savings and jobs are gained, he said. "I look at this as a battle for the future of America," he said.

For the most part, Grey said he's passed the baton on to the foundation's executive director, Les Bernal, a former staffer for a Massachusetts state legislator. Now it's mostly Bernal, not Grey, who is mentioned in newspaper stories with datelines from around the country as the national activist trying to fight gambling expansion proposals.

But Grey hasn't given up the mantle completely. It couldn't be easy to do—especially when you're the David in the David vs. Goliath tale, and you feel your cause couldn't be more righteous. He notes that over the years he's been called a do-gooder, a moral crusader, and his favorite: a wandering religious fanatic. Doesn't faze him a bit.

Grey talks of no one having more "hand-to-hand combat experience" against the gambling industry—and by all accounts, he's right. He speaks with pride about 250 "direct engagements" he's had with the industry. About being outmanned and massively outspent in virtually every fight—and yet still winning a healthy percentage of the time. He talks of the countless trips he's been on, about how he's often been able to afford to take them only because he stays at the modest homes of the activists he meets instead of hotels. He laughed as he noted the surprise he's sometimes caused when being picked up at the airport, ragged suitcase in hand, by locals who may have been expecting a somewhat larger-than-life figure to be striding toward them. "I'm no one," he said. "I'm one of them."

Grey said he remains optimistic, despite the current onslaught of gambling proposals filling the landscape. "The industry claims, 'We're the wave of the future. We're inevitable.' But I know we're winning, because their arguments have collapsed," he said. "There's not a state that's gambled themselves rich."

He paused for a moment. "Stop and think," he said. "They should win 'em all. We're nothing. But we control the countryside. We control the hearts and minds. Our best days are ahead of us."

ACKNOWLEDGMENTS

I'm indebted to my dedicated literary agent, Katherine Fausset, for signing me on and then for sticking with me until we found a great publisher. Many thanks, Katherine. And thanks also to Gayatri Patnaik, my thoughtful editor at Beacon Press, whose suggestions improved this book in many ways. (Of course, any errors of fact or judgment are mine alone.) To everyone at Beacon: I'm forever grateful that you recognized the value of this book.

I've been bending the ear of Keith Whyte with the National Council on Problem Gambling for years about my plans for this book. Thanks Keith. I likewise need to thank everyone who agreed to share their stories with me. To the gamblers, their friends and family, and the many others—the politicians, antigambling activists, gambling industry officials, researchers, and problem gambler advocates—I'm grateful to each of you.

The idea for this book first came to me as I was writing a series of stories about problem gambling for the *Seattle Post-Intelligencer* in 2004. But that series never would have come to pass without the support of my editor, Margaret Santjer. I was working a night police beat at the time, and I needed a backer—an editor to convince the higher-ups at the newspaper that I could somehow do my regular job and write the series, and that the importance of the topic was worth the stretch. Margaret was a steadfast backer, so many thanks to her.

I had many friends at the *P-I* and elsewhere in Seattle who knew of my gambling and my interest in writing about it, and have given me great encouragement. Thanks to Mark Matassa, Kristin Dizon, Mike Lewis, and Richard L., to name just a few.

I wrote my book proposal during my 2007–08 Knight-Wallace Fellowship at the University of Michigan. I loved Ann Arbor, and my time there made this book possible. Thanks to each of the fellows and administrators. Several read my proposal and offered valuable advice—and all were really supportive.

There were others I met during the fellowship who also have been helpful. Thanks to Margaret Lazarus Dean and Chris Hebert for reading my proposal and introduction and for offering useful suggestions, and to Fara Warner for her book-writing guidance.

During my time in Las Vegas, Brendan Buhler, Michael Squires, and others have listened and offered their encouragement as I shared my book-writing travails. Several older friends have been great as well. Thanks to Eric Ellman and to the Vegas trip regulars: Steve Weiss, Adam Lloyd, Jim Allen, Ori Kochavi, and Andy Yarrish.

Finally, I'm lucky to have such a wonderful family. My mom, Sara, and my dad, Marvin, and stepmom, Linda, have been endlessly encouraging. My brother, Josh, has been genuinely supportive throughout the process, and my sister, Abby, likewise has been terrific. Heartfelt thanks to each of them and their kin.

NOTES

Introduction: A Gambler's Journey, and a Country's

1. American Gaming Association Ten-Year Trends Fact Sheet, http://www.americangaming.org/Industry/factsheets/statistics_detail .cfv?id=8.

2. According to Christiansen Capital Advisors' July 31, 2003, *Insight* newsletter, Americans lost $10.4 billion gambling in 1982.

3. Americans spent about $9.7 billion on movie tickets in 2007. http://boxofficemojo.com/yearly/.

4. Kim Clark, "Against the Odds: Gambling Has Become America's Hot Pastime. But Today's Casinos Have More of an Upper Hand," *U.S. News & World Report,* May 23, 2005.

5. I. Nelson Rose, "Gambling and the Law: The Third Wave of Legal Gambling," *Villanova Sports and Entertainment Law Journal* 17, no. 2 (2010).

6. I use the term "gambling industry" throughout the book instead of the industry's preferred "gaming industry" not to make a political point but simply because "gambling" is the accepted term for the actual activity. "Gaming" is not.

7. Howard J. Shaffer et al., "Estimating the Prevalence of Disordered Gambling Behavior in the United States and Canada: A Meta-analysis," Harvard Medical School Division on Addictions, December 1997, http:// www.divisiononaddictions.org/html/publications/meta.pdf.

8. In 1997, Congress charged the National Gambling Impact Study Commission with conducting a comprehensive study into the social and economic ramifications of gambling in the United States. The commission released its final report, which urged state legislators to pause their gambling expansion efforts and made scores of other recommendations in 1999.

9. John W. Welte et al., "The Relationship of Ecological and Geographic Factors to Gambling Behavior and Pathology," Research Institute on Addictions, September 2003, http://spgfoundation.org/Library/Studies%20and%20White%20Papers/Addiction%20and%20Health/welte%20ecological_and_geographic_factors.pdf.

10. Rachel A. Volberg, "Gambling and Problem Gambling in Nevada," Report to the Nevada Department of Human Resources, 2002, http://dhhs.nv.gov/PDFs/NV_Adult_Report_final.pdf. It should be noted here that Volberg used two prevalence screens in her study. See chapter 3 for a more detailed look at the results of both screens.

11. Donald Wittkowski, "Surging Pennsylvania Casino Slot Market Tops Atlantic City for the First Time," *Press of Atlantic City,* January 22, 2010.

12. Jan Murphy and Kari Andren, "Legalization of Video Poker Is Revived to Help Pennsylvania to Pay for Transportation Needs," *Patriot-News,* April 13, 2010.

13. Alex Roarty, "Pileggi Slams Video Lottery," Pennsylvania Legislative Services, August 5, 2009.

14. Associated Press, "States Go All In, Expand Gaming to Plug the Budget," (Syracuse, NY) *Post-Standard,* March 15, 2010, http://www.syracuse.com/have-you-heard/index.ssf/2010/03/states_go_all_in_expand_gaming.html.

15. National Gambling Impact Study Commission Final Report, 1999, Full Report, pp. 1–7, http://govinfo.library.unt.edu/ngisc/reports/1.pdf.

16. Eliza Strickland, "Gambling with Science: Determined to Defeat Lawsuits over Addiction, the Casino Industry Is Funding Research at a Harvard-Affiliated Lab," Salon.com, June 16, 2008, http://www.salon.com/news/feature/2008/06/16/gambling_science.

Chapter 1: The Other Gambling Addicts: The States

1. Paul Galloway, "Shootout in Deadwood: A Homemaker Guns Down Kevin Costner's Bid to Raise a Town's Stake in Gambling," *Chicago Tribune,* June 27, 1994, http://articles.chicagotribune. com/1994–06–27/features/9406270031_1_gambling-interests-deadwood-south-dakotans/2.

2. Ibid.

3. South Dakota Commission on Gaming Annual Report, Fiscal Year 2009, http://www.state.sd.us/drr2/reg/gaming/annual_report/ FY2009%20Annual%20Report.pdf.

4. "Analysis of the Current Markets for Gaming in South Dakota, with Projections for the Likely Impacts of New or Enlarged Facilities," Cummings Associates, April 5, 2004, http://www.state.sd.us/drr2/reg/ gaming/Analysis.pdf.

5. South Dakota Lottery, Fiscal Year 2009 Annual Report, http:// lottery.sd.gov/documents/FY09AnnualReport.pdf.

6. Pamela M. Prah, "States Scramble for Gambling Jackpot," Stateline.org, September 12, 2007, http://pewresearch.org/pubs/591/ states-scrambe-for-gambling-jackpot; Fox Butterfield, "As Gambling Grows, States Depend on Their Cut to Bolster Revenues," *New York Times,* March 31, 2005.

7. Todd Nelson, "S.D. Bankruptcies Down 5 Percent, Judge: Gambling Caused Most Cases," (Sioux Falls, SD) *Argus Leader,* January 15, 1993.

8. Robert Goodman, *The Luck Business: The Devastating Consequences and Broken Promises of America's Gambling Explosion* (New York: The Free Press, 1995), p. 53.

9. Michael Connor, "States Embrace Sputtering Casinos to Plug Gaps," Reuters, August 11, 2010, http://www.reuters.com/article/idUST RE67A3EA20100811?type=domesticNews.

10. Robert Goodman, "Legalized Gambling as a Strategy for Economic Development," United States Gambling Study, March 1994, https://dspace.ucalgary.ca/bitstream/1880/47995/1/Legalized_Gaming _as_a_Strategy_for_Economic_Development.pdf.

11. Prah, "States Scramble for Gambling Jackpot."

12. Michael J. Crumb, "Cash-Strapped States Go All In on Gambling: New Games, Lottery Options, Casinos Planned to Make Up for Revenue Drop," Associated Press, March 15, 2010, http://www.msnbc .msn.com/id/35879023/ns/us_news-life/.

13. Rose, "Gambling and the Law: The Third Wave of Legal Gambling" (see intro., n. 5).

14. Raymond D. Sauer, "The Political Economy of Gambling Regulation," Clemson University, 2000, http://hubcap.clemson.edu/~sauerr/ work/pegambling.pdf.

15. Raymond Sauer, "A Historical Tradition," *New York Times,* July 29, 2010, http://www.nytimes.com/roomfordebate/2010/7/29/should-internet -gambling-be-legalized/the-public-use-of-gambling-revenue-in-hard -times.

16. Rose, "Gambling and the Law: The Third Wave of Legal Gambling."

17. Lydia Saad, "Four Moral Issues Sharply Divide Americans," Gallup, May 26, 2010, http://www.gallup.com/poll/137357/four-moral -issues-sharply-divide-americans.aspx.

18. Jeffrey M. Jones, "Gambling a Common Activity for Americans," Gallup, March 24, 2004, http://www.gallup.com/poll/11098/Gambling -Common-Activity-Americans.aspx.

19. "Gambling: As the Take Rises, So Does Public Concern," Pew Research Center, May 23, 2006, http://pewresearch.org/assets/social/ pdf/Gambling.pdf.

20. The Saint Consulting Group, 2010 poll, Charts and Graphics, http://tscg.biz/the-saint-index/graphics.

21. The Saint Consulting Group, 2010 poll, Executive Summary, http://tscg.biz/the-saint-index/executive-summary.

22. Debate between Frank Fahrenkopf Jr. and the Reverend Tom Grey, October 2006, http://www.youtube.com/watch?v=q74wZkgo7vs and http://www.youtube.com/watch?v=20DRWvMmC90&feature=re lated.

23. National Conference of State Legislatures, "Gambling Developments in the States," 2009–2010, http://www.ncsl.org/default.aspx ?tabid=20222 and http://www.ncsl.org/?tabid=12739.

24. Adam Rose, "The Regional Economic Impacts of Casino Gam-

bling: Assessment of the Literature and Establishment of a Research Agenda," 1998, http://govinfo.library.unt.edu/ngisc/reports/ecoimprpt.pdf.

25. Connor, "States Embrace Sputtering Casinos to Plug Gaps."

26. John Warren Kindt, "The Costs of Addicted Gamblers: Should the States Initiate Mega-Lawsuits Similar to the Tobacco Cases?" *Managerial and Decision Economics* 22: 17–63 (2001), http://www.ideals .illinois.edu/bitstream/handle/2142/16275/Mangl_Decis_Econ_Costs2 .pdf?sequence=2.

27. Sean P. Murphy, "Mass. Casino Backers Playing Numbers Game," *Boston Globe,* June 11, 2007, http://www.boston.com/news/ local/massachusetts/articles/2007/06/11/mass_casino_backers_play ing_numbers_game/.

28. Clyde W. Barrow and David R. Borges, "New England Casino Gaming Update: Patron Origin Analysis and a Critique of its Critics," *Gaming Law Review and Economics* 14, no. 3 (2010), http://www .umassd.edu/media/umassdartmouth/seppce/centerforpolicyanalysis/ negu_a_critique_of_critics-1.pdf.

29. Matthew Teague, "Gaming the System," *Philadelphia,* June 2007, http://www.phillymag.com/articles/gaming_the_system/.

30. Greg Fajt, chair of the Pennsylvania Gaming Control Board, letter to the editor, *Philadelphia Inquirer,* June 25, 2010.

31. William N. Thompson, "Gambling Taxes: The Philosophy, The Constitution and Horizontal Equity," 17 *Villanova Sports and Entertainment Law Journal* 389 (2010).

32. Earl L. Grinols, *Gambling in America: Costs and Benefits* (Cambridge, UK: Cambridge University Press, 2004), p. 33.

33. Paul A. Samuelson, *Economics: An Introductory Analysis* (New York: McGraw-Hill Book Company, 1948), p. 577.

34. Grinols, *Gambling in America,* p. 175.

35. Scott Bland, "Do State Governments Have a Gambling Addiction?" *Christian Science Monitor,* July 17, 2010, http://www.csmonitor .com/USA/Politics/2010/0717/Do-state-governments-have-a-gambling -addiction.

36. Goodman, *The Luck Business,* p. 26.

37. Douglas M. Walker and John D. Jackson, "Do Casinos Cause Economic Growth?" *American Journal of Economics and Sociology*

66, no. 3 (July 2007), http://walkerd.people.cofc.edu/pubs/AJES-growth
.pdf.

38. Monica Yant Kinney, "The Lifeblood of Parx Casino in Bucks Is
Low-Rolling Locals," *Philadelphia Inquirer*, March 7, 2010.

39. Monica Yant Kinney, "Maybe Bensalem's Parx Casino Should
Hire Babysitters," *Philadelphia Inquirer*, September 5, 2010, http://
www.philly.com/inquirer/columnists/monica_yant_kinney/20100905
_Monica_Yant_Kinney__Maybe_Bensalem_s_Parx_Casino_should
_hire_babysitters.html.

Chapter 2: Welcome to Las Vegas, Problem Gambling Capital of the World

1. Nevada Gaming Commission and State Gaming Control Board,
Quarterly Report for the quarter ended March 31, 2010, http://gaming
.nv.gov/documents/pdf/r5_10mar.pdf.

2. Response to written questions by the author from Chris Jones, a
spokesperson for McCarran International Airport, Friday, June 11, 2010.

3. Showboat, Inc., company history, http://www.fundinguniverse
.com/company-histories/Showboat-Inc-Company-History.html.

4. Nevada Revised Statute 463.350, http://www.leg.state.nv.us/NRS/
NRS-463.html.

5. Liz Benston, "Aliante Has Locals in Its Sights," *Las Vegas Sun*,
October 29, 2008, http://www.lasvegassun.com/news/2008/oct/29/
aliante-has-locals-its-sights/.

6. David Strow, "Lavish New Green Valley Casino to Target Locals," *Las Vegas Sun*, December 14, 2001, http://www.lasvegassun.com/
news/2001/dec/14/lavish-new-green-valley-casino-to-target-locals/
?history.

7. Benston, "Aliante Has Locals in Its Sights."

8. Richard N. Velotta, "Q&A: Kevin Kelley, Executive Vice President and COO, Station Casinos," In Business, *Las Vegas Sun*, January
1, 2010, http://www.lasvegassun.com/news/2010/jan/01/q-kevin-kelley/.

9. David Strow, "Study Renews Problem Gambling Debate," *Las
Vegas Sun*, March 25, 2002, http://www.lasvegassun.com/news/2002/
mar/25/study-renews-problem-gambling-debate/.

10. Gamblers Anonymous international meeting directory, http://
www.gamblersanonymous.org/mtgdirTOP.html.

11. R. Keith Schwer et al., "Beyond the Limits of Recreation: Social Costs of Gambling in Southern Nevada" (paper, Annual Meeting of the Far West Popular Culture Association/American Culture Association, Las Vegas, NV, March 20, 2003).

12. Rod Smith, "Problem Gambling's Social Costs High, Report Says," *Las Vegas Review-Journal,* February 13, 2003, http://www.re viewjournal.com/lvrj_home/2003/Feb-13-Thu-2003/news/20669247. html.

13. William M. Epstein and William N. Thompson, "The Reluctance to Tax Ourselves: Nevada's Depravity," *Las Vegas Review-Journal,* May 2, 2010, http://www.lvrj.com/opinion/nevada-s-depravity-92614189 .html.

14. Jane Ann Morrison, "Online Gambling Stories Make Case for Legalizing, Regulating and Taxing," *Las Vegas Review-Journal,* December 8, 2008, http://www.lvrj.com/news/35699879.html.

15. Bo J. Bernhard et al., "The Nevada Problem Gambling Project: Follow-Up Research," University of Nevada, Las Vegas, International Gaming Institute, 2009.

16. *Crime State Rankings 2010: Crime Across America,* Kathleen O'Leary Morgan and Scott Morgan, eds. (Washington, DC: CQ Press, 2010).

17. Richard C. McCorkle, "Gambling and Crime Among Arrestees: Exploring the Link," U.S. Department of Justice Office of Justice Programs, National Institute of Justice, Washington, DC, 2004.

18. Buck Wargo, "Las Vegas Posts Nation's Highest Metropolitan Foreclosure Rate," *Las Vegas Sun,* April 28, 2010, http://www.lasveg assun.com/news/2010/apr/28/las-vegas-posts-nations-highest-metro -foreclosure-/.

19. Peter J. Elmer et al., "The Rising Long-Term Trend of Single-Family Mortgage Foreclosure Rates," Federal Deposit Insurance Corporation, 1998, http://www.fdic.gov/bank/analytical/working/98-2.pdf.

20. Peter Wallsten and Peter Nicholas, "Clinton Plays Gaming Card against Obama," *Los Angeles Times,* January 18, 2008.

21. Steve Green, "Nevada Leads Nation in Rate of Bankruptcy Filings," *Las Vegas Sun,* November 30, 2009, http://www.lasvegassun .com/news/2009/nov/30/nevada-leads-nation-rate-bankruptcy-filings/.

22. Ibid.

23. Kevin Ferguson, "Bankruptcies, Gambling Are Linked in Study," *Las Vegas Sun,* September 11, 2001, http://www.lasvegassun.com/news/2001/sep/11/bankruptcies-gambling-are-linked-in-study/.

24. Associated Press, "Nevada Cities Rank High in Divorce," *Las Vegas Sun,* May 19, 2010, http://www.lasvegassun.com/news/2010/may/19/magazine-2-nevada-cities-rank-high-in-divorce/.

25. Donald W. Black et al., "The Effect of Pathological Gambling on Families, Marriages, and Children," *CNS Spectrums* 12, no. 8 (2007), http://www.cnsspectrums.com/aspx/articledetail.aspx?articleid=1162.

26. Matt Wray et al., "Leaving Las Vegas: Does Exposure to Las Vegas Increase Risk for Suicide," *Social Science and Medicine* 67 (2008).

27. Marshall Allen and Alex Richards, "Elders Deepen Tragedy of State's Suicide Rate," *Las Vegas Sun,* August 5, 2007.

28. Ibid.

29. IHS Global Insight (USA), Inc., Consulting Services Group, "Economic Impact of the Payday Lending Industry," 2009, http://www.cfsa.net/downloads/eco_impact.pdf.

30. Guy W. Farmer, "Gambling Has Been Good for Nevada, but Regulation Is Critical," *Nevada Appeal,* June 3, 2007, http://www.nevadaappeal.com/article/20070603/opinion/106030102.

31. Corporation for National and Community Service, annual "Volunteering in America" survey, 2009, http://www.volunteeringinamerica.gov/rankings/Large-Cities/Volunteer-Rates/2009.

32. *Daily Beast,* "America's Smartest Cities—From First to Worst," October 4, 2009, http://www.thedailybeast.com/blogs-and-stories/2009-10-04/americas-smartest-cities---from-first-to-worst/.

33. Author interview with Tim Christensen, president, Association of Problem Gambling Service Administrators, June 11, 2010.

34. Liz Benston, "Culinary Union Agrees to Wage Freeze," *Las Vegas Sun,* June 20, 2009, http://www.lasvegassun.com/news/2009/jun/20/culinary-agrees-wage-freeze/.

35. David McGrath Schwartz, "Effort to Repeal Nevada's Lottery Ban Clears First Step," *Las Vegas Sun,* March 26, 2009, http://www.lasvegassun.com/news/2009/mar/26/effort-repeal-lottery-ban-takes-first-step/.

36. Mike Sager, "What I've Learned: Oscar Goodman," *Esquire,* December 31, 2004, http://www.esquire.com/features/what-ive-learned/ESQ0105-WIL_Goodman.

37. Sam Skolnik, "NFL Games in City Still a Long Shot," *Las Vegas Sun*, September 9, 2008, http://www.lasvegassun.com/news/2008/sep/09/nfl-games-city-still-long-shot/.

38. Richard N. Velotta, "Advocacy Group Says It's Okay for Casinos to Market to Gambling Addicts: Head of Nevada Council on Problem Gambling Says Efforts Should Focus on Non-gaming Amenities," *Las Vegas Sun*, July 21, 2010.

Chapter 3: The Asian Connection

1. David G. Schwartz, *Roll the Bones: The History of Gambling* (New York: Gotham Books, 2006), p. 15.

2. Shinhye Kang, "Kangwon Land Drops on Korean Plan to Curb Gambling," Reuters, August 20, 2008.

3. Kim Tong-hyung, "Lawsuits Dog Kangwon Land Casino," *Korea Times*, October 14, 2009, http://www.koreatimes.co.kr/www/news/biz/2010/03/123_53530.html.

4. Justin McCurry, "The Endless Lure of Pachinko: Take a Trip through Tokyo's Exciting Plaza Duo. You Won't Be Alone," *GlobalPost*, April 14, 2009.

5. Michael Konik, *Telling Lies and Getting Paid: More Gambling Stories* (Las Vegas: Huntington Press, 2001), p. 115.

6. "Log On, Ante Up: Online Gambling Offers the Greatest Threats and the Biggest Opportunities," *Economist*, July 8, 2010.

7. Amanda Finnegan, "Las Vegas Sands Weighs Name Change to Reflect Global Presence," *Las Vegas Sun*, September 15, 2010.

8. Selina Toy and Annie Wong, "Gambling Among Chinese Adults in San Francisco: The Prevalence of Gambling Behaviors Among Chinese Adults 18 and Over, A Demographic Profile of Chinese Problem and Pathological Gamblers in San Francisco," conducted for NICOS Chinese Health Coalition, 1999.

9. Nancy M. Petry et al., "Gambling Participation and Problems Among South East Asian Refugees to the United States," *Psychiatric Services: A Journal of the American Psychiatric Association online* 54, no. 8 (August 2003), http://psychservices.psychiatryonline.org/cgi/content/full/54/8/1142.

10. Ling Liu, "Casinos Winning Big by Betting on Asians," Associated Press, July 29, 2006.

11. Ibid.

12. William Finn Bennett, "Casinos Target Asian Americans," *North County* (Calif.) *Times,* November 20, 2005.

13. Liz Benston, "Why Vegas Courts China: Growing Chinese Wealth, Relaxed Visa Rules Promise Explosion of Nation's Visitors," *Las Vegas Sun,* February 10, 2008.

14. Gary Rivlin, "Las Vegas Caters to Asia's High Rollers," *New York Times,* June 13, 2007.

15. Adam Smith, "Casinos Aggressively Market to Asian Americans, but Few Services Help Addicts," *Sampan,* October 1, 2006.

16. Ibid.

Chapter 4: The Rise of the Poker Junkie

1. Ashley Adams, "Charity Poker Tournaments," *Card Player,* July 16, 2004, http://www.cardplayer.com/cardplayer-magazines/65540–17–15/articles/14129-charity-poker-tournaments.

2. Timothy L. O'Brien, "Is Poker Losing Its First Flush?" *New York Times,* April 16, 2006, http://www.nytimes.com/2006/04/16/business/yourmoney/16poker.html.

3. PokerPages.com Industry Index, Buy-In—Historical, http://www.pokerpages.com/ppii/buyin.php.

4. Ibid.

5. O'Brien, "Is Poker Losing Its First Flush?"

6. PokerPages.com Industry Index, Entrants—Historical, http://www.pokerpages.com/ppii/entrants.php.

7. Coeli Carr, "Everything You Need for a Poker Party, Save a Winning Hand," *New York Times,* May 1, 2005, http://www.nytimes.com/2005/05/01/business/yourmoney/01poker.html.

8. Cardplayer.com, "Poker Shows on TV," week of May 3–9, 2010, http://www.cardplayer.com/poker-tools/poker-on-tv/2010/05/03.

9. Howard Stutz, "World Series of Poker: Main Event Attracts Second-Largest Field in History," *Las Vegas Review-Journal,* July 9, 2010, http://www.lvrj.com/business/main-event-attracts-second-largest-field-in-history-98079444.html.

10. Jennifer Newell, "Survey Says 10 Million Americans Play Online Poker for Money," PokerWorks, July 31, 2009, http://pokerworks.com/poker-news/2009/07/31/10m-us-players-playing-online-poker.html.

11. Author interview with Justin Marchand, chief media officer for Card Player Media, July 14, 2010.

12. Stephen A. Murphy, "Uncapped No-Limit Poker Begins Today in Florida," *Card Player,* July 1, 2010, http://www.cardplayer.com/poker -news/9351-uncapped-no-limit-poker-begins-today-in-florida.

13. O'Brien, "Is Poker Losing Its First Flush?"

14. David Hiltbrand, "Teens Cut a New Deal for an Old Poker Hand," *Philadelphia Inquirer,* September 7, 2004.

15. Dan Romer, "Card Playing Trend in Young People Continues," Annenberg Public Policy Center of the University of Pennsylvania, 2005, http://www.annenbergpublicpolicycenter.org/Downloads/Adoles cent_Risk/Gambling/GamblingRelease20050928.pdf.

16. Dan Romer, "Internet Gambling Stays Low Among Youth Ages 14 to 22, but Access to Gambling Sites Continues," Annenberg Public Policy Center of the University of Pennsylvania, 2008, http://www.annenberg publicpolicycenter.org/Downloads/Releases/Release_Romer_gambling _nov25_2008/Card%20Playing%202008%20Release%20nov%2025.pdf.

17. Stephen Lemons, "Joe Watson, the Salon Bandit?" *Phoenix New Times,* April 2, 2007, http://blogs.phoenixnewtimes.com/bas tard/2007/04/joe_watson_in_custody.php.

18. Doyle'sRoom blog (Doyle Brunson), May 16, 2010, http://blog. doylesroom.com/doyle-brunson/doyleism-of-the-day-if-you-want-a -place-in-the-sun-you-have-to-put-up-with-a-few-blisters/.

19. Matt Matros, "Time to Actually Learn Game Selection," *Card Player,* April 25, 2007, p. 100.

20. Todd Brunson, "Maniacs Can Be Dangerous!" *Card Player,* April 25, 2007, p. 58.

21. Mike Ferguson, "The Short Eventful Life of Stu Ungar," *Poker Room Review,* February 3, 2010, http://pokerroomreview.com/articles/ the-life-of-stu-ungar/.

22. "The Tortured Champion," *Good Gambling Guide,* http://www .thegoodgamblingguide.co.uk/thisweek/2001/stuungar.htm.

23. Stephen A. Murphy, "Ivey and Dwan's Vegetarian Bet Highlights High Stakes Poker: $1 Million Bet Booked on Ivey's Ability to Stay Away from Red Meat," *Card Player,* March 8, 2010, http://www.cardplayer .com/poker-news/8660-ivey-and-dwans-vegetarian-bet-highlights-high -stakes-poker.

24. Nolan Dalla, "So You Wanna Be a Tournament Pro? Fuhgeta-boutit!" PokerPages, 2003, http://www.pokerpages.com/articles/archives/dalla27.htm.

25. Stephen J. Dubner, "Phil Gordon Answers Your Poker Questions," *Freakonomics* blog, *New York Times* online, April 18, 2008, http://freakonomics.blogs.nytimes.com/2008/04/18/phil-gordon-answers-your-poker-questions/?hp.

26. Ed Vogel, "The New American Dream," *Las Vegas Review-Journal*, May 26, 2006, http://www.rgtonline.com/article/the-new-american-dream-65040?CategoryName=poker%20news&SubCategoryName=.

27. Associated Press, "Judge Rules Texas Hold'em Is a Skill, Not a Game of Chance," *USA Today*, February 19, 2009.

28. North Carolina Court of Appeals ruling, Joker Club, LLC v. James E. Hardin Jr., May 1, 2007, http://www.aoc.state.nc.us/www/public/coa/opinions/2007/pdf/060123–1.pdf.

29. "T. J. Cloutier Interview," *PokerPlayer*, January 2009, http://www.pokerplayer.co.uk/poker-players/player-interviews/8384/tj_cloutiers_las_vegas_tales.html.

30. Brett Collson, "Cake Poker Buys T. J. Cloutier's WSOP Bracelet," *Poker News Daily.com*, January 27, 2010, http://www.pokernewsdaily.com/cake-poker-buys-t-j-cloutiers-wsop-bracelet-7871/.

31. Jeff Haney, "Poker's Iconoclast," *Las Vegas Sun*, November 6, 2007, http://www.lasvegassun.com/news/2007/nov/06/pokers-iconoclast/.

Chapter 5: The Online Fix

1. Angela Balakrishnan, "Anurag Dikshit: High Roller Who Came Late to the Poker Party," *Guardian*, December 16, 2008, http://www.guardian.co.uk/business/2008/dec/16/anurag-dikshit-profile.

2. Nils Pratley, "Earning $58,000 an Hour," Salon.com, June 3, 2005, http://www.salon.com/technology/feature/2005/06/03/online_poker.

3. "95. Anurag Dikshit," Media Top 100 list, 2005, *Guardian*, July 18, 2005, http://www.guardian.co.uk/media/2005/jul/18/mediatop100200587.

4. "#207 Anurag Dikshit," Forbes.com's list of the richest people in the world, 2006, *Forbes*, http://www.forbes.com/lists/2006/10/7XUE.html.

5. Erik Larson, "PartyGaming's Dikshit Pleads Guilty to Web Gambling (Update1)," Bloomberg, December 16, 2008, http://www.bloomberg.com/apps/news?pid=newsarchive&sid=a4X4XSXn4aHw.

6. PartyGaming's Safeguards page, http://www.partygaming.com/prty/en/responsibility/responsiblegaming/safeguards.

7. American Gaming Association Fact Sheet on Internet Gambling, http://www.americangaming.org/Industry/factsheets/issues_detail.cfv?id=17.

8. National Gambling Impact Study Commission report, June 18, 1999, Chapter 5: Internet Gambling, http://govinfo.library.unt.edu/ngisc/reports/5.pdf.

9. Les Bernal, "A Predatory Business," *New York Times,* July 29, 2010, http://www.nytimes.com/roomfordebate/2010/7/29/should-internet-gambling-be-legalized/internet-gambling-is-one-of-the-most-predatory-businesses.

10. Jennifer Newell, "Survey Says 10 Million Americans Play Online Poker for Money," PokerWorks, http://pokerworks.com/poker-news/2009/07/31/10m-us-players-playing-online-poker.html.

11. "Log On, Ante Up," *Economist,* July 8, 2010.

12. "H2 Assesses the Economic Impact (of) Internet Gaming Regulation in the United States," H2 Gambling Capital, April 20, 2010, http://www.h2gc.com/news.php?article=H2+Assesses+the+Economic+Impact+Internet+Gaming+Regulation+in+the+United+States.

13. Eric Pfanner, "Europe Unleashes Online Gambling to Fill Coffers," *New York Times,* July 27, 2010, http://www.nytimes.com/2010/07/28/technology/28eurogamble.html?_r=1.

14. Ibid.

15. Kevin Di Gregory, Statement before U.S. House Subcommittee on Crime, June 24, 1998, http://www.justice.gov/criminal/cybercrime/kvd0698.htm.

16. John Malcolm, Testimony before the U.S. Senate Banking, Housing, and Urban Affairs Committee, March 18, 2003, http://www.justice.gov/criminal/cybercrime/malcolmTestimony318.htm.

17. Nathan Vardi, "Are the Feds Cracking Down on Online Poker?" *Forbes,* February 11, 2010, http://www.forbes.com/forbes/2010/0301/gambling-bluffing-government-internet-web-online-poker.html.

18. Nolan Dalla, "Can New Jersey Legalize Online Poker?" *Bluff,* March 2010, p. 68.

19. Gary Wise, "Time to Party Again," ESPN.com, February 5, 2010, http://sports.espn.go.com/espn/poker/columns/story?columnist=wise_gary&id=4876750.

20. Poll question on online gambling and a link to the results, *The Week,* August 3, 2010, http://theweek.com/article/index/205659/whats -your-opinion-on-legalizing-online-gambling.

21. Fairleigh Dickinson University's PublicMind Poll, "US Public: Keep Las Vegas in Las Vegas," March 11, 2010, http://publicmind.fdu .edu/casino/.

22. Nancy M. Petry et al., "Internet Gambling Is Common in College Students and Associated with Poor Mental Health," *American Journal on Addictions* 16, no. 5 (2007), http://onlinelibrary.wiley.com/ doi/10.1080/10550490701525673/abstract.

23. Gaming Intelligence Group, "Results of Swedish Online Gambling Study Released," October 5, 2007, http://www.winneronline.com/ articles/october2007/swedenresults.htm.

24. National Council on Problem Gambling, "Problem Gambling Study Reveals Highest Risk for Online Poker Players," http://www.ncp gambling.org/i4a/headlines/headlinedetails.cfm?id=100&archive=1.

25. Keith S. Whyte, Testimony before U.S. House Financial Services Committee, December 3, 2009, http://www.ncpgambling.org/ files/public/advocacy/NCPG_Statement_on_HR_2267_12-3-2009.pdf.

26. Mattathias Schwartz, "The Hold-'Em Holdup," *New York Times Magazine,* June 11, 2006, http://www.nytimes.com/2006/06/11/ magazine/11poker.html.

27. Matt Assad, "Hard Time for a Hard Lesson," *Morning Call,* June 29, 2008, http://articles.mcall.com/2008-06-29/news/4126717_1_bank -robber-prison-cell-gambling-addict.

28. Rev. Gregory J. Hogan Sr., Testimony before the U.S. House Financial Services Committee, June 8, 2007, http://financialservices .house.gov/hearing110/hogan.pdf.

29. Jonathan Cheng, "Ante Up at Dear Old Princeton: Online Poker Is a Campus Draw," *New York Times,* March 14, 2005, http://www .nytimes.com/2005/03/14/education/14gamble.html.

30. Annie Duke, Testimony before the U.S. House Judiciary Committee, November 14, 2007, http://judiciary.house.gov/hearings/pdf/Duke 071114.pdf.

31. Ibid.

32. Julio Rodriguez, "Phil Hellmuth and Annie Duke End Their Relationships with UB," *Card Player,* February 9, 2011, p. 14.

33. Play Rush Poker*—the World's Fastest Poker Game! page, Full Tilt Poker, http://www.fulltiltpoker.com/rush-poker.

Chapter 6: Evolving Science, Questionable Research

1. Allan M. Brandt, "From Nicotine to Nicotrol: Addiction, Cigarettes and American Culture," *Altering American Consciousness: The History of Alcohol and Drug Use in the United States, 1800–2000,* Sarah W. Tracy and Caroline Jean Acker, eds. (Amherst and Boston: University of Massachusetts Press, 2004), p. 388.

2. Allan M. Brandt, *The Cigarette Century: The Rise, Fall, and Deadly Persistence of the Product That Defined America* (New York: Basic Books, 2007), p. 167.

3. Frank J. Fahrenkopf Jr., "Promoting Responsible Gaming," speech transcription, American Gaming Association website, August 2, 1996, http://www.americangaming.org/Press/speeches/speeches_detail .cfv?ID=88.

4. Ibid.

5. Author interview with Howard J. Shaffer, director, Division on Addictions, Cambridge Health Alliance, August 25, 2010.

6. "Salary Update: Who Makes What?" *Washingtonian,* May 2009, http://www.washingtonian.com/print/articles/11/155/12389.html.

7. Fahrenkopf, "Promoting Responsible Gaming" speech.

8. Howard J. Shaffer et al., "Estimating the Prevalence of Disordered Gambling Behavior in the United States and Canada" (see intro, n. 7).

9. Glenn Fowler, "Robert L. Custer, 63, Psychiatrist Who Led Treatment of Gamblers," *New York Times,* September 9, 1990, http://www .nytimes.com/1990/09/09/obituaries/robert-l-custer-63-psychiatrist -who-led-treatment-of-gamblers.html.

10. Raja Mishra, "Gambling Industry Link to Harvard Draws Questions," *Boston Globe,* November 6, 2004, http://www.boston.com/news/ local/articles/2004/11/06/gambling_industry_link_to_harvard_draws _questions/.

11. Strickland, "Gambling with Science" (see intro., n. 16).

12. Howard J. Shaffer et al., "Toward a Syndrome Model of Addiction: Multiple Expressions, Common Etiology," *Harvard Review of Psychiatry* 12 (2004), http://www.expressionsofaddiction.com/docs/shaf feretalsyndrome.pdf.

13. David Ferrell and Matea Gold, "Casino Industry Fights an Emerging Backlash: Gambling: Leaders Mount Sophisticated Effort to Protect Interests, as Critics Say Growth Is Creating More Addicts," *Los Angeles Times,* December 14, 1998, http://articles.latimes.com/1998/dec/14/news/mn-54012.

14. Ibid.

15. Sandra Blakeslee, "Suicide Rate Higher in 3 Gambling Cities, Study Says," *New York Times,* December 16, 1997, http://www.nytimes.com/1997/12/16/us/suicide-rate-higher-in-3-gambling-cities-study-says.html.

16. Ferrell and Gold, "Casino Industry Fights an Emerging Backlash."

17. Ibid.

18. Mishra, "Gambling Industry Link to Harvard Draws Questions."

19. John Storer et al., "Access or Adaptation? An Meta-analysis of Surveys of Problem Gambling Prevalence in Australia and New Zealand with Respect to Concentration of Electronic Gaming Machines," *International Gambling Studies* 9, no. 3 (December 2009), http://www.informaworld.com/smpp/content~content=a917430133~db=all~jump type=rss.

20. Volberg, "Gambling and Problem Gambling in Nevada" (see intro., n. 10).

21. Howard J. Shaffer's Expressions of Addiction website, http://www.expressionsofaddiction.com/galleries.htm.

22. Strickland, "Gambling with Science" (see intro., n. 16).

23. Andres Martinez, 24–7: *Living It Up and Doubling Down in the New Las Vegas* (New York: Dell, 1999), p. 193.

24. Mikal Aasved, *The Psychodynamics and Psychology of Gambling* (Springfield, IL: Charles C. Thomas, 2002), p. 27.

25. Aasved, *The Psychodynamics and Psychology of Gambling,* p. 46.

26. Brian Castellani, *Pathological Gambling: The Making of a Medical Problem* (Albany: State University of New York Press, 2000), p. 20.

27. Press release from the American Psychiatric Association, February 10, 2010, http://www.dsm5.org/Newsroom/Documents/Addiction%20release%20FINAL%202.05.pdf.

28. John Gever, "*DSM-V* Draft Promises Big Changes in Some Psychiatric Diagnoses," *MedPage Today,* February 10, 2010, http://www.medpagetoday.com/Psychiatry/GeneralPsychiatry/18399.

29. Benoit Denizet-Lewis, "An Anti-Addiction Pill?" *New York Times,* June 25, 2006, http://www.nytimes.com/2006/06/25/magazine/25 addiction.html.

30. Marc Cooper, "Sit and Spin: How Slot Machines Give Gamblers the Business," *Atlantic,* December 2005, http://www.theatlantic.com/ magazine/archive/2005/12/sit-and-spin/4392/.

31. Gary Rivlin, "The Chrome-Shiny, Lights-Flashing, Wheel-Spinning, Touch-Screened, Drew-Carey-Wisecracking, Video-Playing, 'Sound Events'-Packed, Pulse-Quickening Bandit," *New York Times,* May 9, 2004, http://www.nytimes.com/2004/05/09/magazine/chrome -shiny-lights-flashing-wheel-spinning-touch-screened-drew-carey .html?pagewanted=all.

32. Ibid.

33. Ibid.

34. Karl Taro Greenfeld, "Loveman Plays 'Purely Empirical' Game as Harrah's CEO," Bloomberg, August 5, 2010, http://www.bloomberg .com/news/2010-08-06/loveman-plays-new-purely-empirical-game-as -harrah-s-ceo.html.

35. Ibid.

36. Ibid.

37. Christina Binkley, *Winner Takes All: Steve Wynn, Kirk Kerkorian, Gary Loveman, and the Race to Own Las Vegas* (New York: Hyperion, 2008), p. 184.

38. Ibid.

Chapter 7: A Federal Role, and a Look Forward

1. Budget Overview from the Substance Abuse and Mental Health Services Administration, http://www.samhsa.gov/About/budget.aspx.

2. "Casinos/Gambling: Long-Term Contribution Trends" page, Open Secrets, http://www.opensecrets.org/industries/totals.php?cycle =2010&ind=N07.

3. "Casinos/Gambling: Top Contributors to Federal Candidates and Parties" page, Open Secrets, http://www.opensecrets.org/industries/ contrib.php?ind=N07&cycle=2008.

4. Liz Benston, "Harrah's Thinks It Can Gain from Online Gambling," *Las Vegas Sun,* June 22, 2009.

5. Guy C. Clark, "Gambling and Political Corruption," NCALG

[National Coalition against Legalized Gambling] White Paper, http://www.noslots.com/documents/corrupt.html.

6. Ibid.

7. "AGA Hails Harvard Study That Says Overwhelming Majority of American Adults Have No Gambling Problem," American Gaming Association press release, December 4, 1997, http://www.americangaming.org/Press/press_releases/press_detail.cfv?ID=125.

8. Author interview with Frank Fahrenkopf Jr., September 30, 2010.

9. William Petroski, "Sour Economy Leads Foes to Drop Push against Casinos," *Des Moines Register,* October 13, 2010.

10. David Harrison, "In Tough Economy, Arkansas' Lottery Exceeds Expectations," Stateline.org, July 22, 2010.

11. Lucy Dadayan and Robert B. Ward, "For the First Time, a Smaller Jackpot: Trends in State Revenues from Gambling," Nelson A. Rockefeller Institute of Government website, University at Albany, State University of New York, September 21, 2009.

12. Ron Stodghill and Ron Nixon, "For Schools, Lottery Payoffs Fall Short of Promises," *New York Times,* October 7, 2007.

13. Ibid.

14. Grinols, *Gambling in America,* p. 150 (see chap. 1, n. 32).

15. Goodman, *The Luck Business,* p. 136 (see chap. 1, n. 8).

16. National Indian Gaming Association 2009 Economic Impact Report, http://www.indiangaming.org/info/NIGA_2009_Economic_Impact_Report.pdf.

17. Testimony of Ernest Stevens Jr., chair, National Indian Gaming Association, before the U.S. Senate Committee on Indian Affairs, July 29, 2010, http://www.indian.senate.gov/public/_files/ErnestStevenstestimony.pdf.

18. Grinols, *Gambling in America,* p. 39.

19. Veronica Brown, "Tribal Responsibility," *Tribal Government Gaming,* March 30, 2010, http://tribalgovernmentgaming.com/issue/tribal-government-gaming-2010/article/tribal-responsibility.

20. Tim Giago, "A New Addiction Is Sweeping Indian Country," NativeTimes.com, August 1, 2005.

21. Drew Griffin and Kathleen Johnston, "Military Uses Slot Machines to Fund Overseas Recreation," CNN.com, May 23, 2007.

22. Ibid.

23. Diana B. Henriques, "Temptation to Gamble Is Near for Troops Overseas," *New York Times,* October 19, 2005.

24. Southern Baptist Convention's Ethics and Religious Liberty Commission, Issues and Answers page, Gambling, http://erlc.com/article/issues-answers-gambling/.

25. The Church of Jesus Christ of Latter-day Saints: Gospel Topics, Gambling, http://lds.org/ldsorg/v/index.jsp?locale=0&sourceId=c9bb2f 2324d98010VgnVCM1000004d82620a____&vgnextoid=bbd508f54922d 010VgnVCM1000004d82620aRCRD.

INDEX

adaptation theory, xvii–xviii, 149, 151

"Addiction and Technology: A Comprehensive Public Health Approach to Understanding the Internet and Internet-Related Disorders" (Shaffer & bwin), 148

Addiction by Design: Machine Gambling in Las Vegas (Schüll), 153

Adelson, Sheldon, 73

Alabama: gambling legislation in, 14

alcoholism: compared to gambling addiction, xxiii, 137

Aliante Station, 35–37

American Gaming Association (AGA), xxiii, 13, 46; funded research, 131–32, 136–39, 152

American Psychiatric Association, xxiii, 137, 156

Annenberg Public Policy Center, 102

Aristocrat Technologies, 53

Arizona: gambling legislation in, 14–15; health study in, 43–44

Arkansas: gambling legislation in, 15

Asia: gambling history in, 68–70; gambling market, 70–73, 99

Asian Americans: Asian Americans United, 81; as casino employees, 81, 83; Drug Abuse Program, 78; fastest growing ethnic group, 67; gambling statistics, 74–76, 81; "generational debts," 68; in New York, 86; problem gamblers, 66–68, 71, 73–75, 82–87, 89–91; in San Francisco, 77; San Francisco poll, 73–74; susceptibility to gambling, 65, 67–68, 74; targeted